THE
HAPPY
RAINMAKER

Praise For *The Happy Rainmaker*

"This short yet profoundly impactful book is destined to leave a lasting mark on the legal profession. For far too long, lawyers have been told they must sacrifice well-being for professional success. This is an exhausting false choice that has simply been accepted as inevitable. In this wonderfully-written parable, Jennifer Gillman dismantles that myth with clarity, warmth, and hard-won insight. Through the fictional journey of senior associate 'Bob' and his wise mentor 'Polly,' she illustrates how it's possible to thrive professionally without burning out personally. By the final page, Bob isn't just surviving Big Law; he has become the fulfilled, high-performing, genuinely happy rainmaker the title promises.

If you are in Law School, a new associate just staring out and trying to find your footing, or a seasoned lawyer who feels perpetually drained by the demands of the job, pick up the book, read it, study it, embrace the principles and suggestions, and begin applying them immediately. And if you're a parent, grandparent, spouse, or friend of someone considering or already in the profession— buy this book and place it directly into their hands. Few gifts are as thoughtful, timely, or potentially life-changing. *The Happy Rainmaker* isn't just good. In an industry notorious for burnout, it's urgently necessary."

—**Bob Burg**, Award-winning coauthor of *The Go-Giver*

"*The Happy Rainmaker* feels like a lifeline for attorneys who've forgotten what joy at work feels like. Jennifer writes with a sincerity that reaches you right where you are."

—**Jeff C. West**, Award-winning coauthor of *The Hidden Heist*

"*The Happy Rainmaker* is an energizing and timely guide that speaks directly to the heart of attorney wellness and sustainable success. Jennifer brilliantly offers practical strategies for building a thriving practice without sacrificing mental health, balance, or purpose. As a past President of the New Jersey State Bar Association who founded and organized the Putting Lawyers First task force that surveyed, studied, and confirmed we are a profession in crisis as well as the reality that the pace of the practice is not sustainable, I deeply appreciate how clearly the book aligns with our mission to support lawyers as whole people, not just professionals. I highly recommend it to any attorney looking for a healthier, more fulfilling path to growth and congratulate Jennifer on authoring a masterful must-read."

—**Jeralyn Lawrence**, Past President, New Jersey State Bar Association, Past Chair of the Family Law Section of the NJSBA

"I highly recommend *The Happy Rainmaker* by Jennifer Gillman for any attorney seeking to build sustainable success without sacrificing personal well-being. Through an engaging business fable and practical six-pillar framework, Gillman offers a refreshingly honest roadmap for developing both a thriving practice and a fulfilling life—proving these goals aren't competing forces but complementary strengths. Her approach resonates deeply with The Free Lawyer® philosophy: you don't have to choose between professional excellence and personal freedom when you build the right foundation."

—**Gary Miles**, Founder, The Free Lawyer

THE
HAPPY
RAINMAKER

A Little Tale About A Lawyer Who
Found Success And Happiness Too

JENNIFER L. GILLMAN

INDIE BOOKS
INTERNATIONAL

THE HAPPY RAINMAKER
A Little Tale About A Lawyer Who Found Success And Happiness Too

The views and opinions in this book are those of the author at the time of writing this book, and do not reflect the opinions of Indie Books International or its editors.

Neither the publisher nor the author is engaged in rendering legal or other professional services through this book. If expert assistance is required, the services of appropriate professionals should be sought. The publisher and the author shall have neither liability nor responsibility to any person or entity with respect to any loss or damage caused directly or indirectly by the information in this publication.

The 6 Pillars To Be(coming) A Happy Rainmaker, LLC™ is a pending trademark of Jennifer L. Gillman and Gillman Strategic Group.
Gatorade® is a registered trademark of Stokely-Van Camp, Inc.
Oreo® is a registered trademark of Intercontinental Great Brands, LLC.
Fitbit® is a registered trademark of Google, LLC.
Advil® is a registered trademark of Haleon US IP LLC.
LinkedIn® is a registered trademark of LinkedIn Corporation.
YouTube® is a registered trademark of Google, LLC.
ESPN® is a registered trademark of ESPN, Inc.
Golden State Warriors® is a registered trademark of Golden State Warriors, LLC.
NBA® is a registered trademark of NBA Properties, Inc.
Kansas City Chiefs® is a registered trademark of Kansas City Chiefs Football Club, Inc.
NFL® is a registered trademark of NFL Properties, LLC.
Super Bowl® is a registered trademark of NFL Properties, LLC.
Mets® is a registered trademark of Sterling Mets, L.P.
Knicks® is a registered trademark of New York Knicks, LLC.
iPhone® and Apple® are registered trademarks of Apple, Inc.
Google® is a registered trademark of Google, LLC.
Amazon® is a registered trademark of Amazon Technologies, Inc.
Forbes® is a registered trademark of Forbes LLC.
Law.com® is a registered trademark of ALM Global Properties, LLC.
Law360® is a registered trademark of Portfolio Media, Inc.
Trader Joe's® is a registered trademark of Trader Joe's Company.
Starbucks® is a registered trademark of Starbucks Corporation.

This is a work of fiction, an approach the author is using to impart business lessons. Names, characters, businesses, places, events, and incidents are either the products of the author's imagination or used in a fictitious manner (except for cited books and articles and famous locations included for atmosphere). Any other resemblance to actual persons, living or dead, or actual events is purely coincidental. The use of any actual location is not a sponsorship or endorsement, but just an effort to give the work an authentic feel.

ISBN-13: 978-1-966168-64-5

Designed by Melissa Farr, Back Porch Creative, LLC

INDIE BOOKS INTERNATIONAL®, INC.
2511 WOODLANDS WAY
OCEANSIDE, CA 92054
www.indiebooksintl.com

Table Of Contents

Are You A Bob BigLaw, Sam Solo, Or Suzy SmallLaw?

For twelve years, I was a practicing attorney, and I'm still very type A. I bought into the myth that if you work harder, you'll get better results.

Now that I own my own legal recruitment business, it's really important to me to help as many unhappy lawyers as I possibly can. However, much like some of the lawyers that I care about, I don't always make time for personal appointments.

I wrote this novella for all the lawyers like three of my fictional characters: all the Bobs who work for big firms, all the solo practitioners like Samir (Sam), and all the attorneys at small firms like Suzy.

You all deserve health and happiness. Our motto is "Successful lawyers deserve to be happy too."

And Then Something Happened

Some years back, my stomach had been bothering me. I went to my doctor, who said, "Oh, well, you're fifty, you should have a colonoscopy. I'm signing you up for a procedure in six months."

I agreed, thinking that six months was far away.

But, before I knew it, it was the week of the scheduled colonoscopy. That week turned out to be hectic because I was helping a lawyer who already had a job offer through another recruiter, but really wanted to work at a particular big firm's office in Houston, Texas.

Listen To Mom

The firm told us they were going to get us an offer early in the week. Since the colonoscopy was on Friday, the timing should have been fine. But the offer still hadn't come in by the end of the day on Wednesday, and I was thinking I should put off that colonoscopy. That's because once we received the offer, I would have to help with any necessary negotiation and be a resource to the candidate in making the decision.

My mom urged me to keep the appointment. "Honey, after COVID, there is a big backlog of people who need all of these tests done," she said. "If you cancel, it's probably going to be at least six months until you can get another appointment."

Little did I know, heeding her advice probably saved my life.

Getting The Colonoscopy Wasn't Easy

If you know about colonoscopies, you know the prep step is the worst part. For colonoscopy prep, you'll drink a prescribed laxative solution, often mixed with clear liquids like water or Gatorade. I went through the prep on Thursday evening and on Friday morning, and it seemed like no big deal.

But then, while I was sitting at my computer typing emails before leaving for the procedure, I started projectile vomiting. I called the doctor and asked if I should cancel.

The doctor's office said, "No, don't cancel, but go lie down. When this happens, a lot of people end up fainting and hitting their heads."

But Duty Called

Just then, we finally received the offer we'd been waiting for. I texted my candidate and emailed the firm that made the offer. The candidate called me to discuss the offer, and I negotiated. And in between, I was still throwing up.

I finally told my candidate I had a medical test that I had to go and do. "So, I'm going to be under an anesthetic for just a few minutes, but I'm sure this seems like it's the final offer."

Crossing My Health Crisis Finish Line

Good thing I kept the colonoscopy appointment because they discovered I had stage one colon cancer and had to have surgery. The doctor did say if I had canceled that appointment and waited for their next opening, it could have been a very different story.

Health matters. We always tell our candidates that we work with, "Yes, it's inconvenient for your clients to have you be away from the office for two hours for a cancer screening, but it's even more inconvenient if you have to take six months off to treat the cancer that you didn't catch. And it's extremely inconvenient if you die and they have to work with different lawyers."

To all the Bob BigLaws, Sam Solos, and Suzy SmallLaws out there, the moral of the story is to take care of the important aspects of life. My wish is that this book inspires you to do just that.

Jennifer L. Gillman,
Gillman Strategic Group
Westfield, New Jersey

P.S. My candidate took the offer in Houston and worked happily at that firm for several years. And I remain cancer-free.

PART I

Once Upon A Time There Was An Unhappy Attorney

1

Meet Bob BigLaw, A Victim Of Undeserved Misfortune

B ob BigLaw groaned the groan of an unhappy man.

It was 2:30 a.m. and Bob was still at the office, poring over documents. If he finished soon, he might be able to get a couple of hours of sleep before he needed to be right back here to start on the next brief.

The 6:00 a.m. alarm roused the exhausted lawyer from his slumber, the ache behind his eyeballs an all too familiar feeling. He could tell this was going to be a triple-shot espresso kind of morning.

Bob was unhappy, but it wasn't his fault. He had fallen into a trap that many associates fall prey to. Bob bought into the myth that if you just worked harder than everyone else, it would all work out in the end.

That is a tragic mistake, a seduction of success that can prove fatal to a career and a happy life.

Bob told himself he actually didn't mind the late nights because he absolutely loved being a lawyer; it had been his dream job since he was a child.

Stumbling toward the bathroom past family photos on the wall brought up fond memories of his father sharing his knowledge of the law and instilling in him a desire for analysis and conflict mediation that had served him well. And while his father was a partner at a small, local law firm, Bob's ambitions went beyond following in his footsteps. Bob wanted to work on cutting-edge litigation, and to him that meant being at a prestigious big law firm.

Bob couldn't turn his legal mind off if he tried; it was overflowing with ideas for arguments and new angles for clients. Inspiration struck so often that Bob kept a notepad next to his bed for those middle-of-the-night ideas.

He even got a waterproof pad and pen for his shower, and jotting down ideas was as routine as washing his hair.

All this hard work was going to pay off soon; Bob knew it. He had been excelling at the firm for nine years, and his goal of becoming a partner was in sight. This singular vision to make partner had dictated nearly every decision he made in the last fifteen years and it came with plenty of sacrifices, most notably his complete lack of a social or romantic life.

When Bob joined the firm, he thought he could be a great lawyer and have a social life too. But then he had to start cancelling dates, which caused women to lose interest in him rapidly. More than once, Bob was so exhausted he even fell asleep during a date. That was understandably a deal-breaker.

While Bob wanted to eventually have a family, he knew that he couldn't balance work and dating right now if he wanted to stay on this track. So, the dreams of a future Mrs. BigLaw and children would have to stay as just dreams, for now.

The first stop when arriving at the office was to hit the break room for another coffee and his go-to breakfast of a pack of mini Oreos (bite-sized, so no crumbs on the keyboard) from the vending machine. Bob couldn't remember the last time he cooked a meal; it seemed like he had consisted solely on vending machine food, coffee, and greasy takeout for years now, and it was taking a toll on his body.

Fitness was another thing Bob had pushed to the back burner, a future goal for when he made partner, and finally had the freedom to take even an hour off to hit the gym.

Bob preferred being in the office ahead of everyone and enjoyed the quiet calm before each jam-packed day. But today's solitude was ruined by a familiar voice behind him.

"Morning, Bob. Getting a late start, I see," said his nemesis at the firm, Gunther Gunner.

Bob nodded a friendly greeting to his fellow senior associate while resisting the urge to roll his eyes.

But then Gunther happily filled the silence.

"I got here an hour ago, already done with the McCormick files," said Gunther. "Greg wanted everything on his desk first thing. Do you need any help on your end?"

Greg was Greg Grinder, the partner who took a particular interest in Gunther because he saw him as a chip off the old block. There is a saying that "If you're trying to make partner, you better have a rabbi," or a partner to sponsor you and speak on your behalf. It was clear to Bob that Greg Grinder, Esq., had chosen Gunther as the senior associate he was betting on to make partner.

Gunther's offer to help Bob was less than sincere. Gunther was only interested in making Bob seem less driven and hardworking than himself. As a fellow senior associate, Gunther also had his sights set on making partner, and both he and Bob knew full well that it was extremely unlikely they could both be promoted in the same year, since they were in the same department.

What started as a friendly rivalry had soured. Gunther and Bob came from very different backgrounds. Whereas Bob's upbringing had been comfortable, and his path always clear, Gunther had to fight to even get an opportunity to become a lawyer. Gunther wore the chip on his shoulder proudly, reminding Bob of his privilege whenever he could, and it served as a great motivating force, fueling Gunther's long nights and tireless work ethic. Even Bob had to admit that Gunther worked his butt off, and he knew Greg and the other partners saw it too. So Bob returned to his office and got back to work.

After a 9 a.m. visit to the vending machines, Bob swung by the desk of his favorite legal assistant, Nina Nurture, to say good morning.

Nina had seen everything. She knew everything that happened at this firm. She knew how the lawyers worked. She knew how the inside politics worked, and she was a wealth of information to the people she trusted. She liked Bob. He was always nice, always respectful.

Bob knew Nina was extremely busy, and he was always kind. A lot of times when he was going to get a cup of coffee, he'd ask if she wanted one, and he remembered how she liked it. He also remembered that she had a sweet tooth. Sometimes, when he was getting candy for his niece and nephew, he'd pick up some for Nina, too, and leave it on her desk. He didn't make a big deal about it, but she knew it was from him.

While Bob had a great rapport with Nina these days, he didn't always recognize her full value. As a rookie, he was practically allergic to asking Nina for assistance, keenly aware of how much the partners already put onto her plate. Though he had to admit, some of it was prideful ego on his part, a need to prove himself.

It wasn't until a fateful day when Nina rescued him that it finally clicked for Bob that he couldn't—shouldn't—do everything himself. During one of his many late-night work sessions, a tired Bob hadn't realized he was working off an older, outdated version of the assigned brief. Nina caught the error with only an hour before it was due. For Bob, this felt like a disaster, and as he furiously scrambled to fix it, Nina calmly put a hand on his shoulder, told him to step back, and got to work.

Before Bob's eyes, Nina performed her magic, taking the work Bob had already done and merging it with the updated brief. Not only that, she improved it along the way, massaging the writing to be much clearer than Bob's exhausted late-night version. With minutes to spare, the brief was complete, and the partners never knew of Bob's mistake.

Nina took the opportunity to lay down some much-needed tough love.

"You're too proud, Bob," Nina said. "This is a team, we succeed as a team. Together. You need to rely on other people here, and if you want to advance in this firm, you need to rely on me. You're not weak for asking for help, and trying to do everything yourself doesn't make you a better lawyer, it just opens you up for mistakes."

Bob took those words to heart, and he and Nina quickly became friends. Having Nina as a teammate proved invaluable. Her years of experience with the firm meant she knew every partner's personalities, quirks, and schedules. She shared her wealth of knowledge, and Bob learned about when the partners were having meetings, who was mad at whom, and even what the yearly bonuses would look like. Her office politics savvy gave Bob an edge that kept him ahead of his rival, Gunther.

A notification alerted Bob to a meeting on his calendar with Greg Grinder. Sure, he was a Gunther fan, but maybe this was the meeting Bob had been waiting for. Greg could make or break his career at the firm. He was the person to impress.

Little did Bob realize the shocking good news/bad news that was ahead.

2

The Goalposts Are Moved, It Is Up Or Out

Bob BigLaw had dreamed about making partner for as long as he could remember. And now, after nine grueling years of giving the firm every drop of his time, his energy, and at times what felt like his very soul, he finally heard Greg Grinder utter the words: "Congratulations, Bob. You made partner."

Bob's elation was short-lived, as Greg revealed that there was, of course, a catch.

"It's income partner," Greg clarified, barely giving Bob time to smile. "Being an equity partner is the next goal. You have up to four years to make a business case for becoming an equity partner. If you want a bigger piece of the pie, you need to prove you can make the pie bigger."

Bob couldn't hide the disappointment that flickered across his face, feeling like the rug had been pulled out from under him.

Four more years? The myth had always been that once you made partner, you had arrived.

But this wasn't arrival; this was a different kind of probation. A new finish line drawn even further away. And he could already feel the clock ticking. If he didn't prove himself, the firm would push him out. Up or out—those were the rules.

Greg slapped him on the shoulder. "You'll be fine. Just keep up the hours. Bill sixteen a day if you have to. That's how I did it."

Bob's stomach twisted. Another four years of this? His heart pounded harder just thinking about it. The unhealthy late-night dinners, the vending machine breakfasts, the near-complete collapse of anything resembling a personal life. Was this really it?

Back in his office, Bob thought about Greg Grinder. Greg had been built in the image of the typical service partner, totally focused on executing client work others had brought in. It was all bill, bill, bill, live in the office, die for the firm. His apartment was just a place to collapse between marathon 16-hour stints at the office. No decorations, no family, just a coffee maker and a half-stocked liquor cabinet. Greg had already had a heart attack, but refused to follow the doctor's orders to exercise more and lose weight. He wouldn't even see a dentist, and could barely chew from the tooth pain he stubbornly ignored.

Early in his career, Greg had tried his hand at rainmaking and failed miserably. His awkward attempts to socialize at a networking event caused him to feel humiliated and say to himself, "Well, I'll never do that again." Greg thought rainmaking was for the gifted few. Being a rainmaker was something you were born into, like senior partner Peter Peoples.

Greg's entire identity was tied to billing hours. As Bob considered Greg more, he realized with a growing sense of dread that he was looking into his own potential future.

Nina stepped in, immediately sensing the tension in the air.

"I was going to offer a celebratory drink, but you look like you need something much stiffer," said Nina.

Bob exhaled. "Nina, I don't know if I can do this."

"Buck up, Bob," she replied gently, but firmly. "You know the game here. You can't do it alone, and you can't see the full picture from inside this building."

Bob gave a half-hearted shrug.

Nina continued. "So you're going to take three meetings. I already put them on your calendar."

He opened his mouth to protest, but she knowingly continued before he complained.

"First," she said, ticking off on her fingers, "you're going to talk to your friend Sam Solo, you remember him, right? Your friend who left Big Law Firm to open a solo practice. Then Suzy SmallLaw. Your friend who avoided the world of big firms for a smaller practice. And finally, you're meeting with Peter Peoples."

Bob looked surprised. "Peter? You were able to get a meeting with him?"

Nina smiled. "Peter owes me. He gives an automatic 'yes' for whatever I ask. You know that."

Bob sighed, a mix of gratitude and dread washing over him. Nina was right—he needed perspective. If anyone could help him figure out how to survive this next stage of his journey, it was the people who'd been through it before. Bob once again pushed past his discomfort of asking for help and prepared himself for his three meetings.

Grabbing Coffee With Sam Solo

As long as Bob could remember, Samir Solo went by the name of Sam. He had Bob meet him at a coffee shop near the courthouse, a regular spot for fellow professionals. The noisy place was filled with battered briefcases and exhausted public defenders. Sam looked almost exactly the same as he had in law school, though perhaps a bit more wrinkled around the eyes. Bob had to admit, solo practice seemed to agree with him.

"Bob!" Sam clapped him on the back. "Heard you made partner!"

Bob nodded, not sure whether to laugh or cry. "Income partner."

Sam raised an eyebrow. "Ah. The old moving goalposts trick."

Bob sighed. "Yeah. Four more years for equity. And only if I keep hustling."

Sam leaned back, studying him. "Look, man, I went out solo because I couldn't stand those games. You know what? I make less money, sure, but I get to choose my clients. I control my hours. But if I am honest, I lose a lot of sleep because I am the only one here to do the work. With great freedom comes the great responsibility to get everything done for my clients. I don't think you're going to find what you're looking for in the big law world . . . but honestly, Bob, I'm not sure you'll find it going solo either."

Sam well remembered those law school conversations with Bob. Sam knew Bob's burning desire was to do the highly important cases that only came to a big firm.

Bob sighed but nodded. He knew what Sam was saying was true, but it was strange for someone else to see something in Bob he hadn't fully grasped himself. If solo wasn't the answer, what was? He left the first meeting less sure of himself than before, but he still had two more people to meet.

Catching Up With Suzy SmallLaw

Suzy looked harried when Bob met her in the lobby of her small but well-appointed firm. She'd always been ambitious—smart, funny, unstoppable in moot court—but now she was a partner juggling a family, a toddler, and a practice that was bursting at the seams.

"Bob!" She hugged him tight, then pulled back. "You look—tired."

He gave a humorless chuckle. "Says you."

She rolled her eyes. "Fair. So—income partner?"

"Yeah—I'm a little disappointed to be honest," replied Bob. "And when I see you, with your family, I'm starting to think maybe I should have pursued small practice like you did."

Her face fell. "Ugh. Bob, yes, I avoided that scene so I could have a family. And I do—but my nanny raises my kid most of the time. My husband is a lawyer too, so we're always working. My partners all work in different practice areas. They can't even cover for me when I'm buried. I thought a smaller firm would fix everything, but it just moved the problems around. Bob, I'm not sure big or small law is going to get you the life you want."

Bob's heart sank further. If Suzy couldn't make it work, what hope did he have? He didn't feel too excited for his third meeting, but Nina's reassuring smile and firm push on his back urged him onward.

Ascending To The Lofty Heights Of Peter Peoples

Peter Peoples's office was legendary—enormous, corner views, practically a monument to senior partnership. Bob walked in, nerves jangling. Peter, surprisingly warm, gestured to the visitor chair.

"Nina says I should talk to you," Peter began. "And Nina gets what Nina wants."

Bob laughed weakly.

Peter went on, voice serious. "Bob, let me cut right to the chase here. You don't want to be Greg Grinder. You really don't. Greg is going to die young, and no client is going to show up at his funeral. I've seen it happen before. Remember Bernie?"

Bob nodded gravely, "Sure, he had a heart attack, right?"

Peter's usually warm expression darkened, and he shook his head, "That's what the firm said. They didn't want to tell everyone Bernie took his own life. Suicide is not uncommon in this profession."

A chill ran down Bob's spine, his face paling.

Peter leaned forward. "Don't worry, we're not gonna let that happen to you, Bob."

"Nina says I should just buck up," said Bob.

"She meant buck up until you talked to me," responded Peter. "Believe it or not, I didn't always know what I know, Bob. I had someone help me, a teacher. They call her the Happy Rainmaker. She taught me how to build business *and* stay happy. You can meet her. I'll cash in a chit to get you a conversation. Polly the Professor; you know, Polly, she's of counsel here, teaches at NYU Law now."

"Polly? With the big office at the end of the hall? I see the name on the door, but I've never seen anyone inside," said Bob.

Peter smiled. "Yeah, that's her. She still brings in so many clients the firm won't take her name off the door, even if she's never here."

Bob sat back, trying to process. "The Happy Rainmaker," he thought. "Was that even real?"

"And Bob, I say this because I care," continued Peter. "Get some sleep before the meeting and don't have a breakfast of Oreos out of the vending machine in the break room."

Bob's ears burned, but he managed a smile. For the first time in what felt like forever, he saw a flicker of hope.

As Bob exited Peter's office, the hope turned to dread. Would he measure up when he met a legend like Polly?

3

Enter The Mentor:
The Happy Rainmaker

Bob was fifteen minutes early, but he still felt late for this predawn meeting.

He adjusted his tie for the third time as he stood in front of the doors of Polly the Professor's office. It was uncommon for Polly to even be on-site, and Bob was acutely aware of the rarity of this opportunity.

He hesitated in front of the threshold of something that felt monumental. Not just a meeting, but a moment. Nina had told him to expect a different kind of lawyering here—something transformational.

The door swung open just as Bob lifted his hand to knock.

Polly stood in a coral silk blazer and matching wide-leg pants, a bright turquoise necklace resting just above her collarbone like a crown jewel. She looked entirely at ease and completely in charge.

"Bob," she said, smiling warmly. "Come in. How do you take your coffee?"

The office had almost as much personality as Polly's outfit—mid-century furniture, huge windows that brought in natural light, and pops of color from bold paintings that hung like statements. On the walls were framed photos of her many vacations from around the world. The decor gave a whimsical air to the space, yet Bob still managed to feel intimidated.

On a table near a pair of comfy chairs in the corner, a French press filled the room with the scent of hazelnut coffee.

Bob blinked. "You weren't kidding about coffee."

"I never kid about coffee," said Polly. "Sit."

As he obeyed, she poured them both coffee and sat across from him. Her eyes sparkled, but there was steel underneath.

"So, you want to climb Mount Everest."

Bob paused with his drink halfway to his lips. "Excuse me?"

She gestured toward him with her mug. "You told Peter that your finish line was being an equity partner here at the firm and happily married with a family. That's not a weekend hike. That's Everest."

Bob put his mug down. "Well. Yeah. That's the goal. Peter did it. You did it."

Polly leaned back, amused. "Do you know how many people say they want that and never make it? They burn out. They give up. They break themselves trying. And the ones who do make it? Half of them are miserable."

Bob looked down. "I don't want to be Greg Grinder."

"Good," she said crisply. "Then let's not make you into him."

She reached into a leather folder beside her and pulled out a single sheet of paper. "Here's your offer, Bob."

He took the sheet. It wasn't a contract, at least not in the traditional legal sense. But it felt binding all the same.

It read:

THE EVEREST MENTORING AGREEMENT

Mentor: Polly the Professor

Mentee: Bob BigLaw

Term: Series of six monthly agreements

Lesson Plan: The 6 Pillars To Be(coming) A Happy Rainmaker

Preamble: The general purpose of this Everest Mentoring Agreement is to establish and maintain a productive relationship between the mentor and the mentee, to provide for ongoing means of communication between the mentor and the mentee, and to ensure the swift disposition of grievances the mentor has with the mentee. If the mentee performs the tasks the mentor requires, the agreement will continue for six separate monthly agreements. If the mentee fails to perform the tasks to the mentor's satisfaction, the agreement shall be terminated. Each month, the mentor will instruct the mentee on one of the 6 Pillars To Be(coming) A Happy Rainmaker.

Below that, the six pillars were listed in neat serif font:

- Pillar 1. Care For Yourself

- Pillar 2. Develop Business

- Pillar 3. Define Boundaries

- Pillar 4. Plan Intentionally

- Pillar 5. Learn Continuously

- Pillar 6. Design Your Legacy

Scan to take the
6 Pillars Quiz

"I'm offering to be your mountain guide," Polly said. "But I don't take just anyone up the mountain."

Bob stared at the list. "This looks—doable. But six months of hard work? That's a big ask."

Polly set her coffee down with a soft clink. "You've already spent over a decade between law school and working here, working like your life depends on it. This is six months that will actually change your life."

He shook his head slowly. "I don't know if I can do this. I've already been giving it everything I've got."

"No," she said firmly. "You've been giving everything you've got to them. This? This is giving to you."

"Won't Gunther beat me because he'll keep billing hours while I spend six months on this?" asked Bob.

"I know you were both made income partners and you feel like you are in competition," said Polly. "I also know Gunther has decided to do it Greg's way and just bill until he drops."

"What will happen if my billable hours drop below Gunther's?" Will he be chosen over me?" asked Bob.

"Yes, if billable hours were all that mattered, but they are not," replied Polly. "Rainmakers are prized like rare gems. And Peter and I feel you are a diamond in the rough."

Bob looked up, unsure. "What if this is too much for me?"

"This is an offer," she answered. "You accept, or you don't. The consideration? You give me your time and your commitment. I give you my mentorship. My knowledge. The entire playbook of how I climbed this ridiculous mountain without losing my soul."

Bob sipped his coffee. "What if I breach?"

She turned. "You won't. Because if you're not in it, I won't waste either of our time. This only works if you *want* it."

There was a long pause. Bob looked out the window. The sun was rising, and the New York skyline shimmered.

Bob looked up. "What if I'm not cut out for it?"

Polly smiled, but it wasn't gentle. "Then you'll find out. And that will be a gift too."

Bob considered Polly in all her self-realized glory and compared her to himself. "I'm not sure I can pretend to be someone I'm not."

He watched as Polly walked to the sideboard and returned with a small photo in a frame. It was her, much younger, in a navy blue suit and pearls, hair pulled tight. Standing beside her was her father, proud and beaming.

"My dad was a lawyer," Polly said softly. "Used to quiz me on Supreme Court cases at the dinner table. Told me, if I wanted to be in this game, I needed to understand *how* men did business, *where* they did business, so he gave me golf lessons. I was terrible at first. But I stuck with it."

She laughed at the memory.

"I started reading the sports page, keeping up with politics, and learning to talk about what the clients wanted to talk about. It's not about pretending. It's about learning the rules of the game so you can *choose* when to follow them, and when to rewrite them."

Bob felt something stir. A strange mix of inspiration and unease.

Polly leaned forward. "Do you know why they call me the Happy Rainmaker?"

He shook his head.

"Because I was the one who brought in the clients *and* smiled while doing it. I made business fun. More human. And I never had to become someone I wasn't."

"Nina says you made it all look so easy," Bob uttered quietly.

Polly nodded. "And that's the trick. It *wasn't* easy. I just trained for it. That's what I'm offering you."

Bob let the idea sink in. After his meetings with Sam and Suzy, he was feeling more lost than ever. Here was an opportunity to be mentored by someone not just succeeding in her career, but thriving in ways Bob had begun to write off as impossible for himself.

Bob felt dizzy again. But this time, it wasn't dread.

It was possibility.

Bob signed the agreement with a flourish.

As he got ready to leave, Polly stopped him at the door.

"One last thing," she said. "When I first started, I was still wearing those navy blue suits and pearls, hair pulled back so tight I got headaches. I thought I had to be someone else."

She pointed to the painting behind her. A riot of color—oranges, teals, and deep reds. It looked like a sunset exploding.

"Now? I wear pink suits in court and beat the pants off people who still think power means being boring."

Bob laughed.

Polly's expression softened. "Don't wait to be yourself until the end. Build the life you want as you climb. Or else one day, you'll look down and realize the mountain you climbed wasn't Everest. It was a treadmill. And it led nowhere."

Bob looked out over the skyline, the sun just beginning to rise.

"We will meet at my penthouse at 6 a.m. Here's the address," said Polly.

"I'll be there at 5:55," he replied.

Polly smiled, triumphant.

"Good," she said. "This time, you bring the coffee. And how do you like your eggs?"

PART II

The 6 Pillars
To Be(coming)
A Happy Rainmaker

Care For Yourself

Bob arrived at Polly's penthouse at 6 a.m. on the dot with two venti cups of coffee and a bag of donuts from his favorite shop.

"Good morning. Thanks for the coffee. Throw those donuts into the trash and take a seat at the table," said Polly. "Pillar 1 is care for yourself. Your first task today is to eat some scrambled eggs."

Bob blinked. That wasn't what he was expecting.

"A nutrition lesson seems a little basic, doesn't it?" Bob asked.

"Not basic, it's essential," began Polly. "You're fifty pounds overweight, which is extra apparent because that suit doesn't fit you anymore."

Bob looked down at his suit, one of an expensive batch he purchased when he first started at the firm. The jacket strained whenever Bob folded his arms, and it had been a while since he even attempted to button it.

"The reason it's Pillar 1," explained Polly, "is because in order for the rest of the pillars to work, you need to be alive for them, and I'm going to be frank with you, Bob, you look terrible."

Bob shifted in his chair uneasily as Polly served him a plate of perfectly scrambled eggs.

With Polly on board as his career mountain guide, Bob had been excited to get started on training. He wondered if Polly would have him start with developing leads, or perhaps she'd train him on improving his legal arguments.

Not only did Polly think Bob was fat, but she also had a second hard truth to share.

"You look like you haven't slept in six months, Bob." Polly continued. "Your skin is gray, and the bags under your eyes are so heavy they'd make you check them on a flight."

Squirming under the scrutiny, Bob suddenly felt very self-conscious. Was it so obvious to everyone else that he was overworked? Polly placed a comforting hand on Bob's.

"You can't keep going like this, Bob," said Polly. "You're not going to do your best work. You have to think of yourself like an elite athlete."

Bob laughed at the expression "elite athlete." This was a new concept for Bob.

"Clients pay you a lot of money to give them high-level analysis, to really be present, and give your best answers all the time," said Polly. "And just like an elite athlete, you need to take your physical and mental health seriously, and that starts with getting enough sleep and eating healthier."

Bob started to open his mouth in protest, but Polly was on a roll and already a step ahead of him.

"Now, I get it. You work at a big law firm, and you have a lot of deadlines and a lot of demanding clients; your schedule is packed. And I know what lawyers are like, they're perfectionists. And perfectionists often fall into the trap of thinking something like 'Well, I don't have time to train for the marathon, so I'm not going to start my exercise program now.'"

Bob grunted in protest.

"But I only ever go from my apartment to the office, and back. How am I going to squeeze a workout in there?" Bob whined.

Polly took a dramatic pause and then smiled as she spoke.

"Don't overthink it, Bob. You can walk from your office to the printer. You can park farther away when you go somewhere. You can take the stairs one floor. Find the opportunities right there in front of you."

Polly could tell Bob wasn't convinced.

"I know you're very busy, and very stressed, and time is at a premium, but you make a nice living," observed Polly. "You have the advantage of having disposable income, especially since you never have time to go anywhere other than the office. If you stopped spending so much on greasy takeout you could use some of that hard-earned money to hire a personal trainer, or you could hire somebody to prepare meals, or even somebody to do your grocery shopping and stock your refrigerator. There are a lot of things that you can do to remove the friction from the process and make it easier for yourself."

Bob initially scoffed inwardly at the idea of hiring a trainer, or, more embarrassing, someone to go grocery shopping for him! But then he remembered how he had resisted asking Nina for help at first, and how she proved an invaluable resource and support for him.

Polly continued: "Bob, you have already consumed your lifetime supply of doughnuts. It's time to let the other New Yorkers have their share."

Bob had to smile at that barb.

"When you're ordering food with clients or when you're staying late at the office and ordering in, try ordering something healthier sometimes," added Polly. "Nobody is asking you to go vegan right out of the gate, but you can't eat chips out of the vending machine or a greasy burger for every meal for the rest of your life and feel well enough to be a happy lawyer who gives good advice."

Polly wasn't finished.

"Now let's talk sleep: how many hours a night are you getting, Bob?" asked Polly.

"Um, well . . .," Bob faltered.

"That's what I thought," said Polly. "There is a sleep deprivation epidemic in the legal community, and you look like patient zero."

"I'm dancing as fast as I can here," replied Bob.

"Look, there is no way around it, you're going to have to get more sleep," said Polly. "Long term, you cannot get by on fumes like you have been. I'm sure you can feel the effects of this long-term sleep deprivation. Is your stomach always tight from the constant mix of stress and coffee? Maybe it takes a drink or a sleeping pill to finally quiet your racing mind each night, which just makes it that much harder to wake back up each morning."

Bob took another caffeine hit from his venti black coffee with the extra double espresso shot.

"You've got to figure out how to get more sleep," continued Polly. "Look, no one's talking about eight hours every night, but you can figure out how to get *one* more hour. Unless you have a deadline or an emergency or a trial starting the next morning, you can carve out more time than you are now. Of course, there will be times when you'll need to burn the midnight oil, and we'll deal with that, but you can get more rest than you're getting now, and you must. It's the only thing that's going to save your career and your life."

Taken aback, Bob considered Polly's advice. He knew he needed to make some changes, but nobody had ever been this frank with him about his habits. Polly could see she was scaring Bob a little bit and gave a reassuring smile.

"You can do this, Bob, and I'm here to help," said Polly. "For the next month, I want you to show me in a weekly email what kind of real food you've eaten that isn't junk food from the vending machine. And I want to see what kind of movement you've gotten into your day. You'll have to keep a log on your phone, and I want you to map it out for me in the email. Here, take this."

Polly handed a small wristband device to Bob, who studied it curiously. "A tracking device?" he asked wryly.

"It's a Fitbit, Bob," replied Polly. "I want you to wear it so that I can see when you're sleeping and when you're moving, and then we'll go over it."

"And I also want you to make time to go to the doctor," Polly continued, which immediately caused Bob to bristle.

"This is nonnegotiable," declared Polly. "I know that you're not feeling well. You've got some aches and pains that you take a handful of Advil to cover up. Well, now it's time to get that checked out before it's something more serious. And whatever tests your doctor told you you're overdue for, it's time to schedule them. I don't know if you can get them all done within the thirty days of Pillar 1, but you can make sure that you get them all scheduled for times you know you can actually attend. No rescheduling! Can you do that, Bob?"

Bob nodded determinedly, slipping the Fitbit onto his wrist.

Bob Is Assigned Homework

Polly handed Bob a sheet of paper titled "Pillar 1 Homework Steps."

1. **Eat healthier and move more.** Fat and sleepy are not the way to be an elite attorney.

   Eating a healthy diet and moving more offer a wide range of benefits for physical and mental well-being. You need to find ways to move that body, even if it is five-minute walks around the office. Know this: regular physical activity helps prevent weight gain, reduces the risk of chronic diseases, and improves mood.

   You are what you eat. Good food is good medicine. Think more fruits and vegetables, less processed foods. If the vending machine sells it, it is not good for you. A balanced diet provides the necessary nutrients for optimal health and can help prevent or manage conditions like heart disease and type two diabetes.

2. **Create a food journal of exactly what you are eating.** Send it to me in an email every week. Writing it down and knowing you have to share it with me will improve what you eat. What you measure gets managed. A food journal offers several benefits, including improved awareness of eating habits, identifying potential triggers for physical and emotional issues, and aiding in weight management and overall health. If you don't do this, this is a deal breaker. This is also for the entire six months. By tracking what you eat and how you feel, you can develop

a better understanding of your relationship with food and make more informed choices.

3. **Start wearing a Fitbit.** The Fitbit is my gift to you. If you think I did it to keep track of you, you would be right. A Fitbit is a fitness tracker and smartwatch app that monitors and records various health and fitness metrics. That means I will know about your steps, heart rate, sleep patterns, and more. It's worn on the wrist and typically syncs with your smartphone app to display and analyze data, providing insights into your activity and overall well-being.

4. **Get a physical from a physician.** I want a note from your doctor that you met. No excuses. So jump on this right away because it can be hard to get an appointment. Tell them your work demanded it. Here is why I am insisting on this: Many health conditions, such as hypertension, diabetes, and certain cancers, can develop without noticeable symptoms. The power is in the knowing. Regular physical exams enable healthcare providers to detect these issues early, when they are often more manageable and treatable, leading to better outcomes and potentially increasing survival rates.

   Knowing your health status can provide peace of mind and address any potential health issues promptly, alleviating anxiety and preventing complications.

5. **Start getting more sleep.** Sleep is not an indulgence; sleep is the power you need to be awesome.

Sleep deprivation is an epidemic facing the legal industry. Your body needs sleep to repair itself and your mind. Track how much sleep you are getting nightly and increase it by one more hour for the next thirty days.

Getting more sleep offers numerous benefits for both mental and physical health, including improved focus, mood, and immune function, as well as potentially aiding in weight management and reducing the risk of chronic diseases. Sleep also plays a crucial role in memory consolidation and learning.

6. **Read the book *Managing The Professional Service Firm* by David H. Maister.** Professor Maister, formerly of Harvard Business School, wrote several bestselling books that are beneficial for lawyers. This classic will provide insights for the next pillar.

"If you do not provide me weekly emails of your progress, then our deal is terminated," Polly said firmly. "I expect integrity from you, Bob. Integrity is doing what you said you are going to do. Repeat back to me your understanding of our agreement."

Like a schoolchild answering his teacher in a flat monotone, Bob restated Polly's Pillar 1 deal points from his homework assignment.

"Great!" Polly beamed. "I'll see you for breakfast one month from today. Remember, 6 a.m. sharp. Oh, and I have a three-strikes law. You only get three strikes and you are out."

Develop Business

Bob arrived at 6:05 a.m. Today he brought a bag of baby carrots.

"You're late, Bob," said Polly, "That's strike one."

Bob instantly knew Polly was deadly serious about those three strikes.

"First, may I pay you a compliment?" asked Polly.

Bob was taken aback. "I can use all the compliments I can get."

"Bob, you look healthier already," said Polly. "Your food journals show you are eating better, the Fitbit tells me you are moving more, and the note from the doctor proved to me you are a mentee of his word."

"Thanks, Polly, it wasn't easy," replied Bob.

"Let's begin. The second pillar of becoming a happy rainmaker is to build your own book of business, to have your own clients," said Polly. "Oh, and it never gets easier, you just get better at it."

Bob let out a little groan.

Polly ignored him and proceeded. "Business development is crucial to your legal career for two key reasons. First, the book of business gives you power over your career. Second, it allows you to practice law at a higher level by providing meaningful, impactful advice to clients."

"My dad used to say, 'Follow the golden rule,'" recounted Bob. "'The people who bring in the gold get to rule.' But how do you find the time?"

"As the ancient Greeks used to say, 'it's about buying out the opportune time,'" said Polly. "This means finding time at the expense of something else. It may seem daunting, but it becomes much more manageable when you think of it as a long-term endeavor that compounds small actions."

"I wish the professors at law school taught this," said Bob, who then realized he was talking to an NYU law professor.

"Yes, guilty as charged," sighed Polly. "The problem is that law school doesn't prepare you to build your book of business. When I first started practicing law, I had no idea it was so important. I thought that doing excellent legal work would be enough to guarantee my success."

"Someone once told me, 'Just do excellent legal work and the rest will take care of itself,'" said Bob.

"They may have lied to you about other things, too," chortled Polly. "While you should do excellent legal work, having your own book of business makes or breaks your career."

Bob took a deep whiff of the aroma coming from the oven.

"Sit down, Bob, your egg white and veggie casserole will be ready in a flash," began Polly. "Now, pop quiz: Are you a grinder, a minder, or a finder?"

"If I am profitable, does it really matter?" asked Bob.

"I will answer your question with a question: Do you want to be happy?" asked Polly. "Here is your egg casserole. Give me your book report on *Managing the Professional Service Firm*."

Bob took a bite of the eggs, made a yummy sound, and proceeded.

"*Finders, minders,* and *grinders* are terms originally coined by Professor David Maister of the Harvard Business School in his book *Managing the Professional Service Firm*," began Bob. "Grinders are the attorneys who churn out the legal work. They are typically earlier in their legal careers and expected to bill hours. They often are behind the scenes. Minders in a law firm excel at managing a team and overseeing administrative tasks. Their clients 'belong' to another attorney, but they are responsible for day-to-day contact. Finders are the rainmakers. They are always seeking out and generating new business for the firm.

"So, who are the happiest?" asked Bob.

Polly replied, "I prefer the words of the author Larry Winget: 'No one ever wrote down a plan to be fat, broke, stupid, lazy, unhappy, and mediocre. Those are the things that happen to you when you don't have a plan.' Being a rainmaker needs to be a part of your happy life game plan."

"What is the key to lawyer happiness?" asked Bob.

"The short answer is control, because when you are a rainmaker, minders like Greg have to listen to your schedule because you brought in the client, right?" queried Polly.

"Having control seems like the domain of the special few like Peter," said Bob. "He took me to a networking event. That man knows how to work a room."

"And don't tell me that you're not like Peter and you can't bring in clients," said Polly. "Everyone can be a rainmaker. We just have to work with what you have going for you and what's in your skill set. And Peter's not a magician. He does a lot of things in the background to make that work."

"Peter just seems like a natural," opined Bob.

"Yes, Peter happens to really like people, but you seem friendly too," said Polly. "I bet you have a few friends from law school you could take out for lunch. You probably have a couple of clients you like well enough to have coffee with, right?"

"Okay, I object," responded Bob. "Who has the time?"

"Objection overruled," declared Polly. "Every lawyer, from Thurgood Marshall to Ruth Bader Ginsburg, had 168 hours in a week. No more, no less. It is how you use them."

"But meeting people is hard," lamented Bob.

"It doesn't have to be hard," said Polly. "Think about the things that you enjoy anyway. Is there something that you would like to do, something you'd like to volunteer your time for, or a club you'd like to be in, or something that would make you happy anyway? Then you come across as authentic. When you're at the stamp collector's club and you really love collecting stamps, people can sense that. So think about what you like to do, but you've got to make time on your calendar for doing it."

"Seems frivolous," observed Bob.

"You have to treat it as part of your job, Bob," said Polly. "They've told you you've got four years to bring in some significant clients if you want to make equity partner, right?"

Bob pursed his lips and nodded.

"I know what the firm is like," said Polly. "I rose through the ranks there, too. They're probably going to be talking about it at your next review. So, you really have only got a year to show them some real progress."

"A year!" exclaimed Bob. "I didn't know the clock was ticking that fast."

"Don't panic, you have made a start," said Polly, encouragingly. "You've got a year, let's craft that plan."

"Please don't give me that platitude, 'If it's going to be, it's up to me,'" said Bob.

Polly retorted, "I prefer the adage: 'Nothing great was ever accomplished alone.'"

Bob did not look convinced.

"Now, there are some resources at the firm," continued Polly. "Write this down. There's a marketing department you could lean on. You don't have to do everything yourself. You don't have to handle all of the details, so figure out what you want to do. Do you want to go to conferences? Do you want to speak? Do you want to join a networking group? Do you want to meet one-to-one with clients and potential clients? Whatever it is you're going to be doing for business development, get help from the marketing department for it. If you need a slide deck, let them do it. If you need to find a place where you can deliver your speech, let them look for it. Let them make the arrangements."

Bob started feverishly taking notes. He felt like he was back in contract law class with that stern professor right out of central casting.

Polly continued: "You do the things that only you can do. You build the relationships, you're the one who's speaking. Let them set everything up, and you just go there. And once you lean on them, you'll find that you have a lot more time than you thought for rainmaking. And if you're still having trouble feeling confident about it, I'm happy to talk about some techniques with you, and I bet Peter would too."

"Won't Peter see me as needy?" asked Bob. "That's not a good look."

"Peter will be happy to pay it forward, like I expect you to pay it forward one day," replied Polly. "And there are coaches who can do this, too. They will help you create your own marketing plan. They can help you every step of the way. If you wanted help with your backhand in tennis, you would get a coach, right? It's okay to get a coach to help you with your rainmaking."

"Where do I even start?" asked Bob.

"In the next month, I want you to focus on how you're going to build out your rainmaking plan and take some steps to actually do it," said Polly. "When we meet next month for breakfast, I'm going to ask you about it, and you'd better be able to tell me what you did."

Why A Book Of Business Is So Important

Polly explained that it all comes down to economics, as in the study of how things work and why people do what they do.

"Economically, a law firm is a business," said Polly. "A law firm depends on attracting new clients and keeping the current clients happy."

"So, what you are saying is *the law firm* needs to be in the rainmaking business?" queried Bob.

"No, clients don't typically turn to law firms for advice," explained Polly. "Instead, they go to lawyers, and those lawyers work in firms. Even if you work at a big firm, you have to have the mindset that you are in business for yourself. You want to build your personal brand as a lawyer whom clients can trust."

Polly went on to explain that people trust those they first know, like, and with whom they develop relationships. The firm may provide some level of brand support and assurance that a lawyer has access to resources, but clients overwhelmingly choose law firms by choosing the lawyers who work at those firms.

"The more business you bring in, the more important you are to the firm," said Polly. "The more important you are to the firm, the more power you have over when, where, and how things get done. Your book of business determines your compensation, and it's what allows you to determine when and where you work."

"But wait," interjected Bob. "Isn't the adage, 'Time is money'? The firm buys my time by the year and sells it to clients by the hour for profit."

Polly shook her head "no," then took a sip of her coffee from a bright blue and yellow ceramic mug she had brought back from a vacation in Sorrento.

"As an associate, all you can offer a firm is time, so you work long hours set by someone else," said Polly. "That is the hamster wheel you are on—it's the book of business that allows you to escape that."

Polly further explained that there is another advantage to having your own clients: it's how your career evolves from writing briefs to providing meaningful advice.

"Your clients see you as a trusted advisor and come to you with pressing issues that matter to them in their business or life," said Polly.

Polly now had Bob's full attention.

"Your work becomes one of providing advice, engaging with clients on issues, and helping them understand their options," she added.

"So I get to assign the grunt work to the associates and service partners; after all, they only have time to offer and aren't bringing in the business," said Bob.

"By Jove, I think he's got it," chirped Polly in her best Professor Higgins *My Fair Lady* accent. "But when one of those associates or service partners decides to follow your lead, I hope that you'll act as a business development mentor to them, just like Peter and I are doing for you."

How To Build Your Book Of Business

Polly walked over to her credenza to pick up a laminated chart.

"The problem with building a book of business is that it feels like you aren't getting anywhere at first," said Polly. "As an associate, you start by showing up and doing your work. Over time, if that's all you do, you will likely end up frustrated and not progressing in your career."

"Ah, yes, that hamster wheel you spoke about," said Bob.

"However, if you invest and put in additional effort when it feels impossible, you will reap the rewards in a few years," said Polly.

"As sure as the moon follows the sun: no investment, no return on investment."

Polly then showed Bob this chart.

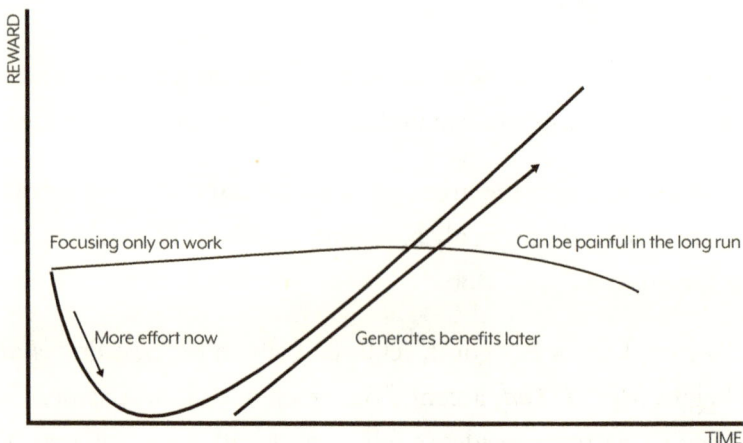

The J-Curve Of Business Development

"Just like Rome, you aren't going to build a book of business in a day," said Polly. "It's like investing: Small amounts invested over time compound to generate much larger rewards later. In the stock market, the investment is money; in business development, the investment is your time."

"This seems like a slow journey, and I have a ticking clock here," complained Bob. "And Gunther is billing a ton of hours."

"Don't focus on competing with anyone else, focus on what you're building for yourself. While at first, it may be slow as you ride the *J* curve down," said Polly, "ultimately, it will become a rewarding journey that not only secures your place in the competitive legal arena but also allows you to align your professional world with your personal goals. You did say you wanted a balanced and fulfilling career as a lawyer and family man, didn't you, Bob?"

Bob thought he was lucky he never had to face Polly as opposing counsel.

"If that is what you want, then potential clients must see you as a trusted advisor, and that kind of trust takes time," said Polly.

Bob Is Assigned Homework

Polly handed Bob a sheet of paper titled "Pillar 2 Homework Steps."

"These are some quick wins you can get this month to start you on the habits of a successful rainmaker," explained Polly. "As David Maister said: 'Rome was not built in a day, but make no mistake about it, we are building Rome here.'"

1. **Do a quick LinkedIn post** where you share your perspective on news articles from law journals, dispel legal misconceptions, opine on legal developments, or write about a recent case and its implications.

2. **Comment on a LinkedIn post** to start a conversation. Maybe someone else commented on the news: what can you add? Comments can be even more powerful than content because they help build a relationship with the person posting. Consider commenting on posts by people who might be ideal clients.

3. **Come up with the topic for an article.** You could go through your emails or text messages and look for

interesting patterns or observations that you could write about. Drafting the article will take more time, but you can jot down your notes and have an associate write it.

4. **Look for a conference.** Attending a conference can be a wonderful way to meet potential clients and get a feel for what is happening in the market you represent.

5. **Reach out to a current client or someone you met.** Regular communication with clients and contacts helps build relationships while keeping you top of mind. Maybe you invite them to lunch or breakfast. (Some rainmakers prefer breakfast because it doesn't interrupt the day.)

6. **Sign up for a networking event** because, like conferences, these can be a terrific way to meet people.

"This seems too loosey-goosey and not strategic enough," said Bob.

"I call that the perfection trap, Bob, and perfection is the enemy of getting started," said Polly. "Many lawyers at the beginning of this journey worry that they will meet the wrong people. But you never know who the people you meet know or how their careers will change and shift."

"But how do I know if the right kind of people are going to show up at networking events?" asked Bob. "This could be a big waste of time."

"Maybe you need to meet corporate leaders who are not going to show up at networking events," said Polly. "But they likely did at one point, so the people you meet now could become future leaders. You may also meet potential referral sources instead of potential clients. Even other lawyers can be a source of business. You need to start making deposits into your relationship bank account."

"The homework seems daunting," said Bob.

"Even seemingly small activities can contribute to making a significant impact," stated Polly. "Also, the people you meet know people, so the people you meet now might know a corporate leader who, at some point over dinner, asks: 'Do you know a good lawyer?' And they will give them your name."

"I agree to give it my best," said Bob. "See you in thirty days."

Define Boundaries

At 5:55 a.m., Bob gently rapped on Polly's door.

"Let the inquisition begin," joked Bob with a smile.

Polly ignored the gentle jibe.

"Let's begin with praise," said Polly. "I have been reading your social media posts, and they're really engaging. Also, Peter said you attended a networking event with him, and he was impressed with how well your suit fit. Good job on the weight loss."

"Ah, just a couple of shovels of snow off Mount Everest," beamed Bob, pleased with his jest—and himself.

"Speaking of snow, tell me what you know about Robert Frost," began Polly without missing a beat.

Bob said, "Frost was an American poet from New England who liked to write about rural life."

"I knew that minor in American lit would pay off one day," thought Bob.

"What did Frost mean when he wrote that 'Fences make the best neighbors'?" asked Polly.

"It is a proverb from one of his poems," replied Bob. "The proverb suggests that establishing clear boundaries between properties helps prevent disputes and fosters better relationships."

"And what does it mean to you when I say, 'Good fences make good lawyers'" continued Polly.

"I think it means I am going to get a discussion about setting boundaries," said Bob.

The Importance Of Establishing Boundaries In Legal Practice

"Yes, Pillar 3 is about defining boundaries," declared Polly. "A lawyer without boundaries is like a garden without a fence."

Bob had a flashback to childhood. He fondly recalled visiting his grandmother's house in New Jersey. She had a big fence around her vegetable garden.

"I get it," said Bob. "Grandma loved her garden and hated groundhogs. Her garden was her pride and joy, but wow, what a few hungry groundhogs could do."

"I thought everyone loved groundhogs?" asked Polly.

"Not Grandma," said Bob. "She used to rant: 'Why can't they just eat one whole tomato and leave the others alone? Why do they have to take a bite out of each one and ruin them all?'"

"Actually, my grandma hated them too," said Polly. "Like a fence around a garden to keep out dreaded pests, achieving a sustainable balance in legal practice requires boundaries too."

Bob asked her for specifics.

"These include delineating your working hours, prioritizing tasks effectively, and learning when to say 'no,'" said Polly.

"Nobody likes to hear 'no,'" observed Bob. "I don't even know where I would start."

"Setting your first boundary has to be something that's authentic to you, something that you really care about," said Polly.

"Give me an example," Bob requested, stifling back a tired yawn.

"Maybe it is making sure that you set boundaries so that you get some sleep," said Polly. "You tell people you set the boundary because 'I only work well when I get some sleep every night.'"

"What if they pressure you?" asked Bob.

"Not if, but when they pressure you," said Polly. "The pressure is coming. You need to say, 'I'm sorry, but that's not going to work for me.' Be firm."

"I think I am going to get push back, especially from partners like Greg, when it comes to activities like exercise," protested Bob.

"Gunther does not 'waste time' exercising. I guess you could say when it comes to exercise, Greg is not a fan."

"You need to show Greg and the clients that your boundaries are part of you being the best lawyer you can be," said Polly. "Phrase it with a *what's in it for them* statement like, 'To be the best lawyer I can be for the firm, I need to get some movement every day. To keep my mind sharp for our clients, I need to fit in time to go to the gym.'"

Polly explained to Bob something she called the option plan.

"Give people options," began Polly. "You can talk to the people you're working with and ask them if it's easier if you go first thing in the morning, last part of the day, or sneak out at lunchtime. But you tell them: 'It's very important for me to be able to do the best legal work for our clients that I get a little bit of exercise.'"

Exercise needs to be daily, not just something you do occasionally on the weekends, explained Polly. Consistency trumps concentrated efforts.

"Exercise is like making the time to floss your teeth: You can't make up for missing daily flossing by picking one day every month to vigorously floss," said Polly.

Bob tried to remember the last time he flossed, but switched back to the conversation at hand.

"The time pressure can be relentless," said Bob.

"You keep telling them, and you have to just say it kindly, but be firm," replied Polly. "Whatever boundary you set—unless it's a true emergency, and those are very rare—you have to make sure that you stick with that boundary."

"What if they know it is something like only a vacation?" asked Bob.

Polly slowly shook her head back and forth to signal "no, no, no."

"When I go on vacation, no one bothers me because I'm on vacation," stated Polly. "Say things like, 'I need to recharge so I can come back more creative and a better lawyer.' You have to talk to people like that. You expect them to agree with you about needing some time-outs from the law."

"But I love practicing law," said Bob.

"You can love the law until it kills you," said Polly. "No doubt you practice law because you enjoy the challenge. It's easy to let the work seep into everything you do; it can become all-consuming."

"Isn't that a little dramatic, Professor?" asked Bob.

"According to the American Bar Association, almost 50 percent of attorneys reported they often work long hours or never stop working. One-quarter said they don't take adequate breaks and nearly one-third said they feel pressured to skip out on vacation time, leading many to consider leaving the profession."[1]

---

1   Debra Cassens Weiss, "Surveyed lawyers report they experience burnout in their jobs more than half the time," ABA Journal, March 9, 2022, https://www.americanbar.org/groups/journal/articles/2022/surveyed-lawyers-report-they-experience-burnout-in-their-jobs-mo/.

"Wait a minute, about half of lawyers are thinking of quitting?" asked Bob. "That seems high."

"Oh, does it?" said Polly. "I knew one lawyer who was a rock-star associate. She billed a substantial number of hours during her first year and then burned out completely because that's what a year of not sleeping will do to you."

Bob knew exactly the associate she was talking about.

"I've heard of more than one lawyer changing their own wedding date because something came up at work," said Polly. "There is a reason lawyers suffer depression at a rate nearly five times that of the general population."

"You paint a bleak picture," said Bob.

"But there is hope," said Polly. "Yes, setting boundaries can be scary. Here is a true story. There was a lawyer in Manhattan who, in open court, stated that she could not make a court date because she'd be on her honeymoon."

"What happened?" asked Bob.

"The judge *and* the opposing counsel congratulated her and happily adjusted the date," said Polly. "They weren't monsters."

"I like a lawyer tale with a happy ending," smiled Bob.

"The moral of the story is you can't have everything all the time," said Polly. "But if you don't set some boundaries, you will make life unlivable and your career unsustainable."

Polly explained that self-imposed restrictions like taking routine breaks, ending work by a specific time, or balancing weekend work with a few free hours during the week become instrumental to one's mental and physical well-being.

"A lack of boundaries affects work-life balance, can lead to increased depression and job dissatisfaction, and can even harm your physical health," added Polly. "Plus, there is no time for family or friends, and that puts you on the continuous apology tour. That means apologizing all day to your clients and all evening to your family, but sadly you won't have to apologize to your friends because they stopped inviting you long ago."

"Been there, done that," said Bob. "And I don't even have a family yet."

"But it's not just about you," added Polly. "If you are overstressed, your work won't be as good. Taking time for yourself allows you to reenergize, change your perspective, and give your subconscious time to digest and solve critical issues, which are good for you and help you serve your clients more effectively. Setting boundaries is good for you, your career, and your clients."

Overcoming The Challenge Of Setting Boundaries Early In Your Career

Polly explained that recognizing the importance of setting boundaries is one thing; implementing them is another.

"The first step for a happy rainmaker involves getting comfortable with the idea that it's perfectly okay and necessary to prioritize your needs," said Polly.

"How does it work in practice?" asked Bob.

"You can't set a boundary that you only work on Tuesdays for an hour, and you don't work the rest of the week," said Polly. "That's not going to work for the firm, but you can set boundaries that you leave at five o'clock every Thursday because you want to coach your nephew's little league team. Every Thursday at five o'clock, you'd better actually get up from your desk and do it, or else people will know that's not a real boundary for you. You can't make up fake boundaries.

"But what can you do if you aren't a rainmaker yet and have limited control over your schedule?" asked Bob.

"The challenge of setting boundaries shifts over the years," said Polly. "As an associate and even as an income partner, since you have less say over your schedule, the challenge is to carve out space and set boundaries where possible. As a rainmaker, you have the *power* to set boundaries; often, the challenge is breaking the habits of the past."

Polly went on to explain that practicing mindfulness could help Bob understand and define his boundaries.

"There is a saying that the body benefits from movement and the mind benefits from stillness," said Polly. "I have found it beneficial to regularly take ten-minute walks to meditate on what is at hand. I call it, 'time to think.'"

"Now you want me to meditate, too?" asked Bob.

"You sound a little judgmental there, Bob," replied Polly. "Meditation is a helpful practice; maybe you want to incorporate meditation. But mindfulness isn't only about meditation. It's about paying attention to what you're doing and only what you are doing in the present moment."

"What should I pay attention to?" asked Bob.

"An important tenet of paying attention is that when something happens, you pause and choose your reaction, rather than reacting automatically," said Polly. "The pause can be a single second, but that one second is an important boundary that allows you to act with intention and in line with your needs."

Strategies For Setting Boundaries As Your Career Progresses

"The best way to ensure you can set more meaningful boundaries is to build a book of business," said Polly. "Once you have a book of business, you set the agenda and can more effectively set boundaries, like how much you work on weekends."

"Not working on weekends sounds like an impossible dream," sighed Bob.

"You may never entirely escape weekend work," said Polly. "But, if you set the agenda, you can minimize it and, when you do work all weekend, you can create some time for yourself during the week. You are the boss of you."

"Polly, forgive me, this all sounds too Pollyannaish," chuckled Bob, pleased with his pun. "I am having a hard time wrapping my mind around this."

"The challenge for rainmakers often comes down to changing your mindset from accepting someone else's priorities to setting the priorities yourself," said Polly.

"I want to believe," said Bob.

"As a rainmaker, know what matters to you and make time for it," said Polly firmly. "I tell many an attorney, 'Your firm should support you regardless; if they don't and you realize that your firm won't let you set boundaries even as a rainmaker, you can find another firm that will. If it does come to that, I know a special recruiter who is a law firm matchmaker.'"

"Tell me more about this matchmaker," said Bob.

"She was a lawyer herself for twelve years and is married to a lawyer at a big firm," said Polly. "She focuses solely on partner-level candidates across the country, and is totally candidate facing, so her loyalty is always with the attorney candidates and not the law firms. But hopefully you won't need her when our work together is finished."

Boundaries Can Be Challenging But Are Essential

Polly had one more topic: the seduction of success.

"It's easy to be drawn into the challenge of work; it can be very rewarding," said Polly. "But if you don't set boundaries, it can be all-consuming, damaging to your health, and even harmful to your clients."

"You make it sound easy, but I am skeptical," said Bob.

"Setting boundaries isn't always easy," said Polly. "It takes effort and can even lead to uncomfortable conversations, but it's also essential for your life and the sustainability of your career."

"Some days I feel so powerless," lamented Bob.

"There are things you can do as an associate or income partner to set boundaries, but the real power comes with a book of business," said Polly. "As a rainmaker, you have the power; the key is to know how to wield it and what you want to prioritize."

Polly handed Bob a sheet of paper with this month's Pillar 3 homework steps.

1. **Plan the work and work the plan.** This month, make time for the things that matter. A plan will help you prioritize. Start by making a list of your priorities. In the next pillar, you will learn to make appointments with yourself in your calendar..

2. **Plan your days.** Plan each day and add a couple of breaks. Schedule a daily meditation. Meditate by focusing on your breathing for six minutes.

3. **Schedule something for yourself every day.** This can be something big or small, but make a point of doing *something* every day. Make the rewards something other than food. Maybe it is watching a funny video on YouTube. Or it could be checking the sports scores on ESPN.com. Perhaps it is a six-minute walk to get some coffee.

4. Plan who you will communicate your boundaries with.
If the lawyer who was going on her honeymoon hadn't *communicated* that she was going on her honeymoon, nobody would have known, and she would have ended up with an inconvenient court date, a missed honeymoon, and an unhappy spouse. Communication was all it took.

5. Buy time for yourself. Hire someone to handle cleaning, meal preparation, or other non-lawyering tasks, which can consume time and prevent you from doing the things that recharge you. This month, ask for a referral for someone who can clean your apartment. Also, ask for a referral for some service or someone to cook meals. You are what you eat. Food is fuel, and you won't go far with inferior fuel in the tank.

Plan Intentionally

B ob arrived early, but waited in the hall before knocking precisely at 5:59 a.m.

"What time did you intend to arrive today?" asked Polly as she opened the door.

"I planned to arrive a little before 5:45 a.m.," replied Bob. "My intent was from the motto you taught me: Early is on time, and on time is late."

"Great answer, because Pillar 4 is 'plan intentionally,'" said Polly. "Last month's homework made you intentional about setting boundaries."

"That homework was harder than I expected," reported Bob. "Choosing your priorities and setting boundaries is not for the faint of heart."

"You are right, Bob, ordinary lawyers don't do it; only extraordinary lawyers make time to think," said Polly. "And thinking is paying off for you."

"What do you mean?" asked Bob, fishing for a compliment.

"In ninety days, you have made noticeable progress," replied Polly. "You've lost fifteen pounds, and I like that new suit. The sleep, exercise, and nutrition plan has improved your appearance and your energy level dramatically."

"Like the old adage: 'Failing to plan is planning to fail,'" said Bob, quoting a Pollyism.

"Allegedly, it was Ben Franklin who said: 'By failing to prepare, you are preparing to fail.'"

"I will look that up," said Bob.

"But you have the right idea, Bob, I do say that because it is easy to fall into a career by default, and there will always be plenty to keep you busy," said Polly. "I want you to plan a long game."

Today Bob was served a parfait of yogurt with granola and fresh fruit.

"When I say *long game*, what does that mean to you?" asked Polly as she took a spoonful of parfait.

"When I hear that phrase, I think of sports franchises," replied Bob. "Particularly in the context of building a successful team over several years."

"Give me some examples," commanded Polly.

"The Golden State Warriors in the NBA took a long game approach to rebuilding, which worked out and resulted in multiple championships," said Bob. "The Kansas City Chiefs are the NFL's most recent example of a successful big picture, long-term strategy, having won three Super Bowls in the last five years."

"You could add what our hometown Mets and the Knicks are finally doing to that list (fingers crossed)," said Polly. "Here's my point: Having a successful career as a rainmaker requires playing the long game. You need a strategy of focusing on long-term results and making intentional decisions with that in mind."

Bob finished his parfait and picked up his pen to make notes.

Polly continued: "A genuinely happy rainmaker builds a career on purpose around their needs and interests. They plan their day to make time for their priorities. Take out your calendar right now, Bob, and let's plan ahead. Show me when your vacation is."

"What's a vacation?" joked Bob. "I think I read about those once."

"Vacations are serious business because they revitalize people," said Polly. "Vacations make us better lawyers. Show me when your vacation is."

"I don't have a vacation on my calendar," admitted Bob. "But I guess I could take off a day for the Fourth of July weekend."

"That's a start , Bob, but show me when you're taking off seven days," said Polly. "I want to see a full week."

"Well, I can't do that in July," said Bob. "I'm too busy. Look what's on my calendar."

"Yes, Bob, that's for that month," said Polly. "Why don't you look six months ahead, which is January? Why don't you look after that trial is finished? Now, block it off 'out of office,' make it so nobody can make an appointment. And then every time you're somewhere with a client or a judge or a partner and they say, 'Oh, that week in January looks good,' you say, 'Oh no, I'm sorry, I'm not available.'"

"You make it sound so simple and easy," said Bob.

"It is simple, but it is not easy," said Polly. "You also need to block off the time that you're going to use for your rainmaking business development activities, like networking and writing articles."

"Don't forget giving speeches and attending conferences," Bob chimed in.

"And all those activities take time, so your homework this month is going to be a written business plan that ties to your calendar," said Polly. "I want to see at least twenty minutes a week for business development activities. I want you to find a networking group that you like, or a conference you want to go to, or some speaking engagements for yourself, and put them on your calendar now."

Polly paused to let Bob catch up with his note-taking.

"And there is more," added Polly. "Whatever it is that you love to do, whether it's working out or joining the knitting club or feeding the homeless or seeing basketball games, I want you to put that on your calendar too."

Polly went to her desk and picked up a replica of a hundred-dollar bill with a portrait of Benjamin Franklin. She handed it to Bob.

"Now turn it over and read the back," directed Polly.

Dost thou love life? Then don't squander time,
for that's the stuff life is made of.
BENJAMIN FRANKLIN

"You need to plan your time intentionally, and that includes properly taking care of yourself," said Polly. "I want you to actually block out sleeping time on your calendar. In the next thirty days, I want you to schedule exercise and doctor's appointments and make sure they are on the calendar."

"Other people can see my calendar, and I don't want them to see gym visits and doctor's appointments," protested Bob.

"And they won't," assured Polly. "For you, Bob, the three magic words in the English language will be: 'out of office.' I want everything that matters to live on your calendar and just to be labeled as 'out of office.' You don't have to tell people what it's for."

Time To Write That Career Plan

"Sometimes I feel my burning desire to make partner is all-consuming," said Bob. "I love the law."

"Even if you love your career and practice area, you can reach a point where your days are not your own, and your priorities become afterthoughts," responded Polly. "That's not a happy way to live your life."

"Planning intentionally is a crucial pillar to becoming a happy rainmaker," continued Polly. "Your homework is not to just think about this, but to write it down in a plan."

"Let's talk about my homework," said Bob. "What goes into this plan?"

"A legal career is a lot like running your own business," said Polly. "You work for a firm, but your value to the firm is highly dependent on the matters you bring into the firm, your book of business."

"But how do happy rainmakers like you and Peter pull it off?" asked Bob.

Polly peeled off another fake hundred-dollar bill and handed it to Bob. He turned the bill over and read another quote.

Drive thy business, or it will drive thee.
BENJAMIN FRANKLIN

"Your reward depends on how well you build your business and serve your clients," said Polly. "You can have a lucrative career and enjoy family and friends, but wishing won't make it so."

Polly declared the career plan starts with three big questions:

- *What is your wealth goal?* How much money do you want to make? What is your net worth goal?

- *What is your freedom goal?* What does freedom mean to you? How do you want to spend your time?

- *What is your impact goal?* What impact do you want to have on the legal industry? In what area of law and niche do you want to be the recognized expert authority?

"Planning is about you and what you want," said Polly. "Even if you're happy where you are, creating a plan can help you grow, expand your network, and discover opportunities."

"I've always thought career planning was about big goals, like making partner," said Bob.

"While macro planning is excellent for steering your career, more is needed," said Polly. "That more is your calendar. Monthly, weekly, and daily planning is how you make sure you set boundaries and make time for your priorities. This includes better nutrition, better sleep, and better exercise. You should also include feeding your mind."

"Who has time to feed their mind?" questioned Bob.

"Remember, you find the time, which means sacrifice," replied Polly. "I recommend listening to audiobooks. And I have a recommendation for your planning. It's a book from *National Geographic* called *The Blue Zones* that contains research on people who control their time so they live longer, fuller lives."

"Most days, I don't feel like I control my life," observed Bob.

"It's true, rainmakers have a lot more calendar flexibility, but making a weekly plan and using your calendar will help throughout your career," said Polly. "And there's no time like the present to get started."

Polly handed Bob a sheet of paper titled "Pillar 4 Homework Steps."

"Bob, your homework is to create a business plan for your career," said Polly.

1. **What are your goals outside of work?** Think romance, family, fitness, spirituality, and fun.

2. **What annual meetings or conferences do you want to go to?** Choose at least three. Put them on your calendar.

3. **What groups do you need to connect with?** Choose at least three. Put meeting dates on your calendar.

4. **Who do you want to meet, and when do you want to meet them?** Choose at least ten. Put inviting them to meet as an action item on the calendar.

5. **What articles do you want to publish?** Choose at least three. Put on your calendar the times to draft articles, or

better yet, times to jot down some notes so an associate can draft them.

6. **What types of cases or news do you want to comment on?** Choose at least three. Put time on your calendar to do this.

7. **What influencers should you connect with?** Choose at least three. Put time on your calendar to reach out to them.

8. **When will you schedule time to take care of yourself?** Book time on your calendar for sleep, exercise, doctors' appointments, vacations, family time, and other commitments that will make you a better lawyer and a happy rainmaker.

Learn Continuously

B ob showed up at 5:59 a.m. at Polly's penthouse with a basket of succulent Rainier cherries, the premium, sweet, yellow cherry with a red blush.

"Just as you requested, a basket of Rainier cherries," said Bob.

"Oooh, yummy, 'Nature's candy,'" said Polly. "Did you know that God did not invent the Rainier cherry?"

'No, I did not know that," said Bob. "Pray tell, who did?"

"I do not know who, but I know how," said Polly. "Scientists in the 1950s at Washington State University learned how to cross a Bing and Van cherry to create a delicious, albeit seasonal, treat. They learned how to do it."

"I feel a pillar coming on," said Bob, with a smirk.

"Pillar 5 is 'learn continuously,'" said Polly. "Learning continuously allows you to keep up with change, keep your advice relevant, and better engage your clients."

Polly served Bob a cut-up apple, a handful of cherries, and a baked egg and veggies muffin cup.

"Did you play sports in college, Bob?" asked Polly.

"No, I figured if God had wanted me to exercise, would he have given me this body?" joked Bob.

"Actually, your workouts and healthy eating are doing you a world of good, Bob," said Polly. "Your clothes are fitting much better, and is that another new suit?"

"So far, I have released twenty pounds back to the wild," declared Bob. "Little habits like taking the stairs or parking farther away add up, too."

"Your Fitbit is testifying to that added exercise," said Polly. "You are looking sharp."

Bob blushed a little.

"Speaking of exercise," said Polly, who retrieved from her desk a framed photo of herself as an undergrad on the Princeton crew team.

"Hey, look at you in the racing shell," said Bob. "I bet those were some cold mornings out on the river."

Polly said: "There is a saying I like that reminds me of the crew team: 'Learning is like rowing upstream: not to advance is to drop back.'"

"So, if I am not keeping up, I am falling behind?" asked Bob.

"Bingo," said Polly. "The last twenty years have touched every industry and every legal practice in one way or another. Even in cases where the law hasn't changed much, your clients' questions, concerns, and understanding of the law will have changed."

"Sure, you have to earn your CLE credits, but is going all-in on learning really necessary?" asked Bob.

"President Harry S. Truman liked to say: 'It's what you learn after you know it all that counts,'" said Polly.

"Touché," said Bob.

"Merci beaucoup," replied Polly. "A legal career can easily last forty years or more. So, when you are twenty years out of law school, you are near the midpoint of your career. That day is coming for you, Bob. Now, think back over the last twenty years and ask what's changed in the law for your clients and in the market your clients work in."

"I get your point," said Bob.

Polly took out her iPhone and said, "Let's ask the oracle known as Google what some of the biggest changes have been in the last twenty years."

Polly let Bob read the AI summary:

The invention of the iPhone and the full embrace of smartphone technology (and all of its privacy implications).

The Great Recession of 2007–2009 and the changes to financial regulation that resulted.

A global COVID-19 pandemic that transformed how people work.

Social media came into existence and changed how people stayed connected and informed.

Blockchain technologies and *cryptocurrency* came into existence.

The introduction of *AI* and *large language models* to the general public.

"As busy as the last twenty years were, the next twenty years will almost certainly bring even more change at an even faster pace," said Polly.

Polly took a well-thumbed book off her shelf, *Future Shock,* by Alvin Toffler.

"More than fifty years ago, Toffler said: 'The illiterate of the 21st century will not be those who cannot read and write, but those who cannot learn, unlearn, and relearn,'" said Polly.

"This would make me more interesting at a party, if I ever went to a party, but will this really make me a better rainmaker?" asked Bob with a hint of skepticism in his voice.

"Crucial to becoming a happy rainmaker is giving good advice to your clients; you must be their trusted legal advisor," said Polly. "That means you must stay ahead of their changing needs and perspectives."

Embracing Change: Why Stagnation Is A Lawyer's Worst Enemy

"Heed this stagnation warning: Your clients exist within a continuously changing environment," said Polly.

Polly took another well-worn book off her bookshelf: *The 7 Habits of Highly Effective People* by Steven Covey.

"But there's more: Continuous learning keeps you sharp," said Polly. "In his *7 Habits of Highly Effective People* book, Covey called his seventh habit 'sharpen the saw.' He and others have done research showing that continuous learning improves critical thinking and problem-solving skills."

"Oh, I get it, mental stimulation that exercises the mind," said Bob.

"There is even some suggestion that continuous learning or mental stimulation can help prevent dementia, which seems like a good enough reason to keep learning all by itself."

Bob suddenly turned somber. That dementia comment hit close to home.

"My grandma had dementia at the end; that is not a good way to go," said Bob. "I hear what you are saying."

Polly took a moment to grasp Bob's hands.

Keep Up With Change, Learn To Understand Your Clients Better

Polly instructed Bob to take another deep breath and let it out. Bob smiled at Polly, telling her he was ready to continue.

"Continuous learning is not just about staying updated with the latest technological trends or legislation," continued Polly. "It's also about understanding your clients and their needs more deeply. That is an investment that pays dividends in the long run."

"Is this the old 'The more you learn, the more you earn' adage?" asked Bob.

"Not exactly," said Polly. "My point is, as you grow from an associate to an equity partner, your contacts are also moving through hierarchies in their firms. This growth means that conversations, challenges, and questions they will have will change as well."

"I don't want to get left behind," said Bob. "That would be really terrible."

"Precisely, you don't want to become mentally obsolete," replied Polly. "Your client may start as a start-up and grow to a multibillion-dollar enterprise; the challenges they face will shift dramatically with that growth. Consider the lawyer Jeff Bezos must have first hired when working on a plywood desk in a garage: that lawyer would have to learn a lot to keep up with Amazon's transformation. Or Steve Jobs' first lawyer at Apple."

Polly handed Bob a laminated photo of Apple founder Steve Jobs with the quote: "Learn continually. There's always 'one more thing' to learn!"

"When you're doing your rainmaking activities, find out what issues are coming up for prospective clients," instructed Polly. "Is it AI that they're worried about? Are they worried about the trade laws? Whatever it is, make sure that you keep up on what's bothering your clients, but also make sure that you keep up on the industry in general, and if things aren't going very well in your own specialty area, then you're able to pivot."

"You make learning sound like career insurance," said Bob.

"That's right, learning continuously separates the best lawyers from the average because it keeps your advice relevant, timely, and focused on your clients' needs," answered Polly. "Here is an excerpt from a blog I wrote on the subject."

Polly hit 'print' on her computer and handed Bob a page.

The Advantages Of Learning Continuously

In addition to helping you keep up with the market, better develop business, and provide relevant advice to your clients, learning continuously will help you:

Feel more confident in your career and advice: the more you know, the more confident you will feel.

Adapt to a changing market: if you have to shift your career (see planning intentionally), a practice of learning continuously will give you the edge and help you adjust.

Be more satisfied at work: research shows that people who learn continuously are happier at work.

Gain insights that you can use to author papers, articles, and posts.

Bob Is Assigned Homework

"It's easy to fall into the trap of thinking you are done with school, but that is a mistake," said Polly. "The world will not stop changing, so staying relevant requires that you keep learning."

"Don't ask a barber if you need a haircut and don't ask a professor if you need to go to school," observed Bob.

"There are many ways to learn continuously, from formal study to reviewing the headlines," said Polly. "It often has the added benefit of putting you in the same room as your prospects, which will always help with business development."

"Sounds like night school to me," chuckled Bob.

"Then I am not doing a good job explaining that continuous learning takes many forms," replied Polly. "It is essential that your learning extends beyond the CLE courses you are required to take. CLE is helpful, but you'll need to do more. This month, you will write a plan for learning continuously."

"I know the drill," smiled Bob. "Lay it on me."

Polly handed Bob a sheet of paper titled "Pillar 5 Homework Steps."

1. **State the advantages of learning continuously.** List in rank order the advantages you see of being a lifelong learner.

2. **What courses will you take in relevant areas?** Try to choose your required CLE credits in areas that will help you. And don't limit yourself to just CLE credits; consider taking other courses, too. These can be online courses, in-person lectures, workshops, or other formats.

   Taking a course in your client's field has the added bonus of getting you in front of more potential clients—you are learning more and meeting more of the right people.

3. **What industry conferences will you attend?** You can learn a lot by listening to the talks at conferences, and you will be in a great position to meet prospective clients.

4. **How will you keep up with the news?** There are free daily news digests you can receive from sources such as the *Daily Skimm* newsletter or *Forbes Daily*, and your firm probably has a subscription to Law.com or Law360 for legal industry news.

   Pay close attention to the headlines and changes in your clients' industry or business area. This helps you stay on top of trends and keeps you up-to-date with industry gossip so that when you meet with your clients, you can speak their language and know what's happening.

5. **Who will you seek out to ask questions?** As highly trained professional experts, lawyers often want to have the answer rather than ask questions. But when it comes to industry knowledge or industry changes, asking your clients for more detail shows you're interested, allows them to be the expert for a while, and gives you inside information. Every piece of industry information you learn from one client becomes knowledge you can use with other clients.

Explain the Chinese proverb: "A person who asks is a fool for five minutes. A person who never asks is a fool for life."

6. **What books will you read?** Reading about an industry or changes in the industry will keep you informed. It can also be an excellent way for self-care (maybe you are reading on a beach or in a park). Your brain is the sum of the books you read. Wise people from Benjamin Franklin to Warren Buffett have expounded on the value of reading.

Design Your Legacy

B ob knocked at 5:59 a.m. with an eighteen-egg carton of Trader Joe's best organically fed, free-range chicken jumbo eggs. The carton had a big red bow and a thank-you card on top.

"Like you said, Polly," Bob said, offering the gift, "if food is medicine, buy the best medicine you can afford. Thank you."

"Your progress is thanks enough, Bob," replied Polly. "But you can open up that bottle of champagne for our mimosa toast."

"What are we toasting?" asked Bob.

"Don't be coy," said Polly. "Peter told me how you brought in a big client that one day could grow to over a million dollars in fees a year. Tell me the evolution of how that happened."

"Well, I met him at the networking event a few months back, and he invited me to speak to the local chapter of the industry association he was chair of," began Bob. "They also asked for a newsletter article on my topic. At that event, a member of the association, a general counsel for a Fortune 500 firm, asked if he could pick my brain over coffee. After the coffee date, we were invited to present to the management team. Peter coached me, but let me quarterback the meeting."

"Bravo," said Polly. "Now let me whip up some veggie-stuffed omelets as we talk. I hope you are giving appreciation gifts to your legal assistant, Nina, too. Without Nina, we never would have had these mornings together."

"Oh, don't I know it," responded Bob. "I used to be afraid to give her work because she was so busy. Now I know that nothing great was ever accomplished alone. I make sure to give her small gifts now, and plan to share the wealth even more when I become an equity partner."

Polly looked up from the omelet pan and gave Bob a big smile.

"Practicing law is not a solitary exercise; you need teammates like Peter and Nina," began Polly. "No lawyer is an island. You will always have to deal with clients, other lawyers on your team, opposing counsel, judges, and juries, too."

"Is that all?" smirked Bob.

"Actually, no," said Polly. "Sometimes, you must deal with the media, regulators, and politicians. There are differing degrees, of course: Writing a contract does not often put you in front of a jury, but the law always involves people, their issues, and a need for agreement of some sort."

"Sometimes I feel I am in the disagreement business," observed Bob.

"If you view it as the agreement business, you will develop a book of business as you become a rainmaker, which means deeper relationships and higher degrees of trust," said Polly.

"Why does this relate to business development?" asked Bob.

"Because you will develop a reputation whether you like it or not," replied Polly. "When it comes time for you to retire and move on—which will happen, I know—you'll need to know what you want from retirement, what you want to leave behind, and how you want to transfer trust and relationships."

"You really are talking about the long game again, aren't you?" asked Bob.

"Yes, this is the very long game, and that's why I call this sixth pillar 'design a legacy,'" said Polly. "For legacy, it's crucial to define your career as a happy rainmaker."

Two Lawyers Walk Into A Courtroom

Polly continued the lesson for the day: "Two lawyers walk into a courtroom."

"Is this a joke?" smiled Bob.

"Far from it," said Polly. "Imagine you are one of the lawyers who walk into a courtroom. You've prepared your arguments, you actually got some sleep, and you ate that perfect energy-filled, but not heavy, breakfast. You are ready."

"Okay, I get the picture," said Bob. "Sounds like an episode of *Law & Order.*"

"The opposing counsel approaches you," continued Polly. "His father, who lives in another state, is in the hospital. Your opposition doesn't know how serious the situation is, but he wants to put off the start of the trial for a week to sort out issues for his father. He wants to know if you'll oppose his request."

"Should I oppose?" asked Bob.

"You have a choice," said Polly. "His father is alive, the situation doesn't sound life-threatening, and you've worked hard to be ready for this moment. You also know that the judge is likely to side with you if you object to the delay, and that would put the opposition off his game—this could be an advantage for you."

"My job is to win for my client, so pressing my advantage has its appeal," said Bob.

"On the other hand, your opposing counsel is human, and his father is in the hospital," said Polly. "What do you do? Here's your omelet, let's discuss."

"Let me weigh the pros and cons to determine the correct answer," said Bob.

"There is no correct answer to the scenario," said Polly.

"I believe there is always a correct answer," replied Bob.

What You Do Is Who You Are

"You could push your advantage or grant the delay; neither's wrong," said Polly. "But your decisions will affect how others perceive you: lawyers, judges, colleagues, and clients. Whether or not they are there in that room, they are listening, and then next time this comes up, someone will tell the story of your actions this time."

"My friend Sally calls that a *karma bomb*," said Bob. "What goes around comes around."

"Sally is right," observed Polly. "The question is: What story do you want them to tell? Do you want to be the ruthless, nerves-of-steel litigator who presses every advantage? Or the empathetic lawyer who will do the right thing? Or something else entirely?"

"I thought you said there was no right answer?" said Bob.

"You have to decide what the right answer is for you, Bob," said Polly.

"Are we talking legacy or reputation here?" asked Bob.

"When you first start your career, designing your legacy means thinking about how you want others to identify you within your professional sphere," said Polly. "It also means acting according to how you want to be perceived so that you build the reputation you want."

"This sounds like the Stephen Covey habit of 'begin with the end in mind,' opined Bob.

"That's right, and bonus points for reading the books I am giving you," said Polly.

"My dad used to say, 'You gotta learn more to earn more,'" said Bob.

"I concur with your dad," responded Polly. "Let's get back to reputation. As your career progresses, your attitudes might change, and your brand can be tweaked, but maintaining consistency is crucial. You can't be a 'scorched-earth, it's-my-way-or-the-highway' lawyer for years, then expect others to bend when you need it. How did Sally describe that karma bomb?"

"'What goes around comes around,'" repeated Bob.

You In Retirement

"Everything ends, Bob," said Polly. "Eventually, retirement will come. I've met many lawyers who believe they will work forever, but whether we like it or not, all careers end."

"So, the real question isn't whether it will end but how I want it to end," reasoned Bob.

"Let me share a cautionary tale," said Polly. "I have seen many lawyers in their eighties who hang on too long. They do it because they have no family, no friends, and no outside interests. The law firm is all they have. If they do leave, they die within a year."

"That may have been my destiny if I didn't redeem myself," mused Bob.

"Precisely, but I am happy to say some lawyers want to leave the firm and never return because they have an attractive retirement to go to," said Polly. "Others, like me, want to be of counsel so we can generate business and receive compensation while playing golf. Plus, I chose teaching, which I find fulfilling. Maybe you want to work as an advisor, providing the kind of advice that can only come from experience."

"But I just want to make equity partner," protested Bob. "Won't this other stuff sort itself out?"

"Your future is for you to decide, Bob," said Polly. "As your career progresses, define what you want from the future. Avoid the killer *D* words like depression, divorce, doubt, discouragement, and destitution."

"You paint a grim picture," said Bob.

"My point is positive, that anything is possible, but you must plan early to turn the possibilities into reality," said Polly. "And that includes building up a war chest."

"Do you mean like a reserve of funds for waging a political campaign?" asked Bob.

"Exactly, but this is a career campaign because another aspect of planning your legacy is financial planning," said Polly. "And frankly, Bob, you were wasting a lot of money before on restaurant meals, takeout, and minor indulgences to cope with a stressful life."

"But I am getting better," said Bob. "I am on a first-name basis at Trader Joe's."

"That's great, Bob, keep it up," said Polly. "You are investing in your health by using your money for healthy groceries and a nutritious meal delivery service. I applaud the balance. There is wisdom in the saying: 'What you don't spend, you get to keep.' The more money you have saved, the more options you'll have later. Therefore, save early and often, benefit from compound interest, and write your plan for the future."

"I feel a homework planning assignment coming on," said Bob.

"One reason early planning is so essential is that transitions take time," said Polly. "Over your career, you'll create strong relationships with clients who trust you. They'll see you as an expert, and they will value your advice. That only comes with time, reputation, and building relationships."

"Peter once told me, 'Relationships are like money in the bank,' but I did not know exactly what he meant," said Bob.

"Ah, relationships," said Polly. "If you decide to own your practice like Sam and want to sell it, or if you want to keep working in a big firm and want to continue to receive origination payments or maximize the profit of the firm you leave, then you will want to transfer those relationships to someone else," said Polly.

"So, Peter meant relationships are like bankable assets with real value," said Bob.

"Investing in these assets takes time and effort; it can take years to establish the right relationships, so you don't want to put it off," said Polly.

Bob Is Assigned Homework

Polly handed Bob a sheet of paper titled "Pillar 6 Homework Steps."

"Designing a legacy is about deciding what you want to be known for and putting it into action," said Polly. "Early in your career, your legacy is your reputation. Later in your career, it becomes, well, your legacy, what you leave behind. You will earn a reputation, retire in some way, and leave something behind."

"That's so much to think about, I wouldn't know where to start," sighed Bob.

"The main question is: 'Are you doing it on purpose and in a way that serves you?'" said Polly. "You'll always be better off if you set your terms. Spend time thinking through the legacy you want to leave in this homework assignment."

"I feel like this is my final exam with you," said Bob.

"Not final, but defining your legacy is a long-term game," replied Polly. "It's actually more about consistent actions than big actions, and here are some decisions to make in writing right now."

1. **Decide what you want to be known for.** Define in twenty-five words or less. Choose clarity over cleverness.

2. **Audit your actions.** Do your actions align with what you want your reputation to be? What is the gap?

3. **Think about your legacy and what you want to leave behind.** Define in twenty-five words or less.

4. **Open a retirement account and a war chest savings account**, and make regular deposits. There is a wise adage that states: "Compound interest is the eighth

wonder of the world. He who understands it, earns it; he who doesn't, pays it."

Get referrals and hire a financial advisor. At the very least you should have a tax-advantaged savings plan designed for retirement. Also, create a war chest interest-paying savings account. Build it up each month until you have six months' income socked away.

5. **Define your special talent and nurture it.** Use the bullet points below to analyze your special talent. This list could go on for pages; the point is to think about how you want to be perceived. This will make you stand out, and it will also make your work more rewarding because you will focus on what you enjoy.

The special talent baseline is hard work and smart legal insights. But you also want to find your distinct niche within your practice. This is "that thing" everyone comes to you for or knows you for, such as the following:

- Being amazing at research, the go-to person any time someone needs help
- Reading and understanding regulations and their implications
- Critiquing and honing oral arguments
- Calming clients down
- Working extra hours to get something across the finish line
- Always attending networking events (or any events), even at the last minute

- Being great at detail; being the one to proofread documents that need to be accurate

- Being a great writer or speaker

6. You will also eventually **start moving into planning for your succession or retirement**. Your answers to this homework will determine how you engage or prepare the next generation; how you manage, mentor, and support the lawyers who work for you; and even the culture you want to create at your firm. Plan as if your life depends upon it because it does. The questions to answer are the following:

- What do you want to pass on to the next generation of professionals?

- What do you want for yourself in retirement?

- How will you make the transition?

PART III

Crossing The
Happy Rainmaker
Finish Line

The Struggle Is Real

Bob got to work.

With all six pillars in mind, every month he built momentum on his journey toward making equity partner. Peter, Nina, and others made positive comments about Bob's new zeal and fresh outlook.

Over coffee at Starbucks, Nina asked him the secret to the turnaround.

"To say it wasn't easy is putting it mildly," explained Bob. "But the key was taking Polly's advice to heart and approaching it incrementally."

Bob said he made an effort to take the stairs instead of the elevator. Nina smiled because she was often there to helpfully remind him whenever he "forgot" and pressed the down button.

Bob didn't expect the dopamine hit the Fitbit would give him, but checking his wrist and seeing the number rise actually felt good.

The idea of hiring someone to cook meals for him made Bob a little bit uneasy, but he found a solution via a meal prep service that delivers. Every Sunday, a week's worth of healthy meals arrived on Bob's doorstep, which was a good investment in his future health.

And while lean proteins and complex carbohydrates couldn't compare to addicting and delicious Oreos, Bob had to admit that he was feeling the positive effects, and he definitely didn't miss the sugar crash.

For Pillar 2, Bob built his book of business by attending conferences, something he never thought he had space for, because the idea of leaving the office for multiple days sounded ludicrous for any reason. But he worked with Nina, and he incorporated Pillar 3 into the mix, to make the case that he would be a better lawyer by going to these events.

And to Bob's surprise, it didn't take that much convincing. He ignored the grumblings from Greg and Gunther, who perceived his away time as vacation (or burnout, hoped Gunther). Instead, Bob kept his mind on Peter Peoples, remembering the friendly and thoughtful approach he took to every potential client, and he brought as much of that energy to each conference as he could. Peter even put in a good word to a conference organizer, and Bob was chosen to organize and speak on a panel in his specialty area.

None of this came naturally to Bob, so he found himself leaning on Pillar 4 quite a bit. Planning helped not only with major events like conferences, but also with the small things, like taking a break to eat the healthy meals he brought every day. But once something was in the calendar, it stayed there, and so month after month, the new tasks began to become the routine, and Bob could feel himself getting into a groove that felt good.

The senior partners noticed too.

It's not that Bob started bringing in a ton of new clients right away, but even that first one felt monumental. Then Bob brought in a few other matters to the firm and he started to feel more confident he could do it again and again. Those first wins set a precedent, and as a lawyer, Bob knew how important precedents can be. Plus, there was a small thrill that came whenever he met with his first client at the office, knowing his peers could see his skills and confidence growing.

Bob never lost sight of his goal to make equity partner, but it didn't loom over him like a sword of Damocles anymore. Bob was so focused on his new strategies for success that he didn't realize how quickly two years had come and gone.

For a moment, he thought the meeting with Greg on his calendar was bad news, but the grin on Greg's face and the congratulatory handshake the moment he walked in sent a jolt of realization through the lawyer.

"Our newest equity partner! You actually did it, you crazy son of a—excuse me, I mean congratulations, Bob."

Bob laughed and shook his head, "I'm almost as surprised as you. Two years ago I wasn't sure this was even possible."

"Service partners like me need rainmakers to bring in the clients, and you need us to get the client work done," said Greg. "We want to tie you up before someone steals you away from us. Trust me, other firms take notice of a rainmaker. You did it, and you deserve it."

Bob smiled, "Thank you, but I was going to say I couldn't have done it without the support of Nina and Peter, and especially Polly."

"And humble too! Bob, you're an amazing lawyer, and now a growing rainmaker too," said Greg. "You're going to do incredible things here, making the pie bigger and better."

"Those are the words I wanted to hear most of all," replied Bob.

Bob left Greg's office floating on air, then nearly jumped out of his suit when a loud *pop* sounded just next to him. There was Nina, a fizzing bottle of champagne in hand.

"Of course, you already knew," said Bob.

"I've been holding it in for *days*, Bob, this was torture!" exclaimed Nina.

Across the office Gunther made eye contact with Bob, and gave him a head nod of acknowledgment. They both knew Gunther was destined to be stuck in the purgatory of income partner, grinding it out and hoping that one day he might make equity partner.

Bob accepted a flute of bubbly and pulled out his phone to send a quick text message. Nina smiled and lowered her voice.

"Are you telling her now?" asked Nina.

Bob nodded softly, "Just sent a message. I should probably make sure I have a dinner date on my calendar, huh?"

Bob had been playing his cards close to his chest, but something else happened a couple of months back while he was following Polly's advice. He met someone.

It wasn't Bob's intention; he was simply making an effort to socialize and stay in touch with his colleagues. And at a wedding for one of his college friends, Bob met Sara, a friend of the bride, and a former lawyer who now taught law classes at NYU. Bob got to practice some of his continuous learning skills, enthusiastically chatting about their shared passion until the dance floor was empty.

Sharing Some Good News With Polly

When Bob called Polly that evening, he had two pieces of good news. Polly expected the news about making equity partner ("There was never a doubt, Bob!"), But the second piece of info sent Polly into an excited arm wave that made her jewelry clack about.

"I think she might be the one, Polly." Saying that out loud removed any notion of "might" from Bob's mind. His path ahead felt clearer and more sure than ever before.

Each One, Teach One:
Spreading The Happy Rainmaker Message

Three more years after making equity partner, the once unthinkable had become Bob's new normal.

His mornings began not with a frantic dash, but with the quiet hum of domesticity. The aroma of freshly brewed coffee mingled with the sizzle of breakfast as he helped Sara prepare a meal for themselves and their two-year-old daughter, Lily. Who knew sautéed kale could pair well with eggs?

Admittedly, Sara was doing the bulk of the cooking part, but Bob knew exactly how Lily liked her strawberries sliced for her yogurt (length-wise not width-wise, and you better believe it matters.)

The meal prep service had been replaced by shared cooking and the joyful chaos of a toddler's breakfast. Bob's Fitbit still adorned his wrist, tracking steps on morning strolls with Lily in her stroller, or a weekend hike, in addition to the stairs he continued to climb every day.

Bob's professional life was climbing, too. The initial thrill of making equity partner had matured into a deep satisfaction. He was indeed doing amazing legal work at the firm, not just as a lawyer, but as a rainmaker, consistently bringing in significant clients. The six pillars were no longer a conscious effort but an ingrained way of being, flowing naturally into his interactions and decisions.

Bob spread the rewards, too. Nina had often talked about taking a European river cruise with her sister someday. A personal gift from Bob turned that some day into a two-week cruise this year, along with another bonus to make sure she would have plenty of money for souvenirs.

One crisp autumn afternoon, Nina, still Bob's invaluably amazing assistant/confidant, poked her head into his spacious corner office.

"Bob, got a person you ought to meet," she announced, her eyes twinkling. "She joined us as an associate a few years ago after a clerkship with the Second Circuit Court of Appeals."

"That's an impressive item on a resume," said Bob.

"Says she wants to be an equity partner, and also have a family," replied Nina. "Sounds familiar, doesn't it?"

Leilani, a young woman, earnest and a little nervous, stood behind Nina. Bob recognized the fire in her eyes, the same fire that burned so intensely within him. But he also could see that fear and growing fatigue, too, and Bob hadn't forgotten the way those feelings once weighed him down.

Bob leaned back in his chair, his warm smile brightening the room a little. "So, you want to climb Mount Everest, do you?" he mused, looking at the associate.

Her head began to tilt in confusion, but she caught herself and nodded determinedly, "If that's what it takes."

"Well, if Nina says so, I'll be your mountain guide," said Bob. "Let's meet for breakfast tomorrow at my place. How do you like your eggs?"

APPENDICES

The 6 Pillars Be(coming) A Happy Rainmaker

Pillar 1: Care For Yourself
Taking care of yourself physically and mentally makes you a better lawyer and helps you show up better for everyone in your life.

Pillar 2: Develop Business
Having your own clients gives you leverage at your firm and the power to set your schedule, dictate terms, and work however you want.

Pillar 3: Define Boundaries
Setting boundaries gives you time for what matters most to you, and helps you build a successful career that leaves room for a full life.

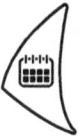

Pillar 4: Plan Intentionally
Taking control of your schedule in the short-term and long-term gives you the ability to fit in the most important parts of your career and life.

Pillar 5: Learn Continuously
Committing to life-long learning allows you to address your clients' evolving needs and adapt to the future of your practice.

Pillar 6: Design A Legacy
Defining what you want to be known for now and in the future and preparing for a meaningful retirement creates a legacy you can be proud of.

Resources From Gillman Strategic Group

I f you've made it to this page, you've followed the journey of a lawyer who realized something powerful: success isn't just about prestige or profits. It's about building a career and life that actually feels good to live.

Now, it's your turn.

To help you take what you've read and apply it to your own path, I've created a set of practical, proven resources just for high-performing lawyers like you.

What Pillars Are Your Strengths?
What Pillars Deserve More Attention?
Take The Happy Rainmakers Quiz And Find Out!

The most powerful first step is finding out exactly where you are today.

Take The Happy Rainmakers quiz to find out which of the 6 Pillars you've mastered and which are your opportunities to grow. Then get access to our curated resources tailored to your results.

Scan here to take the quiz and access your personalized resources:

You'll also get access to:

- **Interactive Workbooks** – Practical exercises for each pillar (What will you do today to care for yourself?)

- **The Book of Business Calculator** – Know your true value by calculating exactly how much business you've generated and what your salary could be.

- **Updated Resources** – Other resources that we grow over time and update regularly

You deserve a career that honors your talent and your life, because successful lawyers deserve to be happy too.

Let's write your next chapter—together.

Acknowledgments

A big thank you to my dad, Barry Gillman, a lawyer who was my favorite human and a significant influence. Also, lots of love and gratitude to my mom, Carolyn Gillman, for always supporting me (and probably saving my life by urging me not to cancel that colonoscopy).

I would like to express my gratitude and all my love to my husband, Drew Kofsky (an attorney himself), and my children, Isaac and Jakob, for their unwavering support and understanding throughout the writing of this book, and always.

Special thanks are in order for the Gillman Strategic Group team and the consultants who've been great supporters of this book project: Jeff Loehr, Laura Castellanos, Amanda Sexton, Stephanie Bushell, Lisa Lunsford, Alphild Rees, Carla Valentin, Todd Gillman, Tina DiMarco, Bobby Shortle, and Jen Hamilton.

I also want to thank Bob Burg for the inspiration that came from the *Go-Giver* series that he wrote with John David Mann. I still bring the original *Go-Giver* book with me almost every time I fly. I would also like to thank everyone who was with me at the Go-Giver Beyond the Mastermind events in January 2024 and August 2025. They helped me see how the 6 Pillars to Be(coming) a Happy Rainmaker and this book could become a reality.

Thanks so much to the business coaches who have helped me reach this point, including Monica Shah and Stacey Brown Randall, with whom I currently work, and Fabienne Fredrickson, with whom I spent several years coaching and who was the reason I met the world's best AB, Anne McGuire.

Thanks to all my sounding board friends and networking contacts who had to hear about this incessantly, and especially all the lawyers who were game enough to try some of the 6 Pillars.

Thanks also to all the lawyers and other professionals who have kindly recorded a Happy Rainmakers video with us for the 6 Pillars resources. They took their own time to do something that they didn't get paid for, and that didn't lead to clients or extra work for them in any direct way. They just wanted to help unhappy lawyers and pay it forward.

I also want to thank Terri Solomon, a rainmaker female partner who showed me that women can do it too, and who I consider to be one of my mentors to this day, as well as Drew Marks, the mentor who helped me get hired at the firm in the first place.

Lastly, I would like to thank my editors and publishers at Indie Books International, including Henry DeVries, Devin DeVries, and Mike DeTuri, for making this dream a reality.

About The Author

Jennifer Gillman is a former practicing attorney turned legal recruiter and founder of Gillman Strategic Group. After more than a decade in law, she saw firsthand that even the most successful lawyers weren't always fulfilled. Today, she helps rainmakers and law firm owners find their exact right, perfect-fit firm, whether that means making a move or merging with another practice.

Her mission is clear: Not one more lawyer suicide, ever again. Successful lawyers deserve to be happy too.

A graduate of NYU School of Law and Brandeis University, Jen blends her legal background with a deep understanding of the profession's pressures to guide lawyers toward careers that align with their goals and values. She is the creator of the 6 Pillars to Be(coming) a Happy Rainmaker framework, designed to support long-term success without burnout.

Jen lives in New Jersey with her husband and two children. She believes the best success stories start with a lawyer finally asking, "What do I really want?"

Let's Connect

Book Jen For Speaking Engagements
Bring the 6 Pillars message to your firm, conference, or bar association.
Email: speaking@gillmanstrategicgroup.com

Order Books In Bulk
Special pricing available for firms, organizations, and events.
Email: info@gillmanstrategicgroup.com

Work With Jen
Ready to find your exact right, perfect-fit firm? Let's talk.
Email: jgillman@gillmanstrategicgroup.com

Follow Jen
LinkedIn: https://www.linkedin.com/in/jennifer-gillman-law-firm-matchmaker/

Website: gillmanstrategicgroup.com